Nathan Oppenheim

The development of the child

Nathan Oppenheim

The development of the child

ISBN/EAN: 9783337215637

Printed in Europe, USA, Canada, Australia, Japan

Cover: Foto ©Suzi / pixelio.de

More available books at **www.hansebooks.com**

THE DEVELOPMENT OF
THE CHILD

THE DEVELOPMENT OF

THE CHILD

BY

NATHAN OPPENHEIM

ATTENDING PHYSICIAN TO THE CHILDREN'S DEPARTMENT
OF MT. SINAI HOSPITAL DISPENSARY

New York
THE MACMILLAN COMPANY
LONDON: MACMILLAN & CO., Ltd.
1898

All rights reserved

COPYRIGHT, 1898,
BY THE MACMILLAN COMPANY.

Norwood Press
J. S. Cushing & Co. — Berwick & Smith
Norwood Mass. U.S.A.

To My Wife

CONTENTS

CHAPTER I
                                                PAGE

INTRODUCTORY 1

CHAPTER II
FACTS IN THE COMPARATIVE DEVELOPMENT OF THE CHILD   11

CHAPTER III
FACTS IN THE COMPARATIVE DEVELOPMENT OF THE CHILD (*continued*) 37

CHAPTER IV
COMPARATIVE IMPORTANCE OF HEREDITY AND ENVIRONMENT 66

CHAPTER V
THE PLACE OF THE PRIMARY SCHOOL IN THE DEVELOPMENT OF THE CHILD 93

CHAPTER VI
THE PLACE OF RELIGION IN THE DEVELOPMENT OF THE CHILD 122

CHAPTER VII

THE VALUE OF THE CHILD AS A WITNESS IN SUITS AT LAW 148

CHAPTER VIII

THE DEVELOPMENT OF THE CHILD-CRIMINAL . . . 175

CHAPTER IX

THE CHILD'S DEVELOPMENT AS A FACTOR IN PRODUCING THE GENIUS OR THE DEFECTIVE 207

CHAPTER X

INSTITUTIONAL LIFE IN THE DEVELOPMENT OF THE CHILD 241

CHAPTER XI

THE PROFESSION OF MATERNITY 266

Φθείρουσιν ἤθη χρήσθ' ὁμιλίαι κακαί

MENANDER

THE DEVELOPMENT OF THE CHILD

CHAPTER I

INTRODUCTORY

ONE of the noteworthy characteristics of the time is the so-called moral revival which has shown itself in almost every part of the civilized world. It has made its imprint upon England, France, Germany, Italy, Spain, and Russia. In our own country it has wrought some striking changes. These changes have been very plainly seen all through the common life of the time, and one of the most interesting features of this revival is the diversity of form which it has assumed. From one end of the social fabric to the other the same note is heard; whether in regard to the subject of dress, or of charity, whether business methods or housekeeping, the spirit of the hour calls for a strenuous effort, a desire to improve upon the past, a noble dissatisfaction that can be quieted only by an active exhibition of individual endeavor. In fact, the keynote of the whole movement seems to be an appeal to the individual to assert whatever energy he has to the end of insuring his best development. The individual is recognized as the ultimate element of the mass, and therefore plans that are meant to improve the mass must begin with each single person. Even in politics, the new-forming touch is felt, and political methods are beginning to take another and newer shape. It is for reasons such as these that M. Charles Secrétan has wisely said: "Political salvation in a democracy depends solely on private efforts, on an inward mission."

One may rightly go further, saying that the salvation which depends upon private efforts, upon an inward mission, is not confined to political life. In fact, in the whole range of human affairs, this sentiment of devotion to the cause of a personal idea, to the cause of an individual belief, is the strongest force that can actuate men. It has the inspiring force that makes martyrs; it begins a crusade, works miracles, incites to heroism. The great captains of all time are the men who have most keenly felt it. The light which radiates from it is so strong that whoever comes into contact with it becomes thereby illumined. It acts as a sort of spiritual infection, whose range of influence extends over the whole race. In times past, when the spirit of the people was more clearly that of a mass, it acted generally from some individual source, from which it spread by waves to surrounding people. Rightly enough, therefore, ancient history was really one-man history, individual history. National and world events meant impulses which originated in one man, or a small group of persons controlled by one man; and whatever force he had was the real motive energy which agitated his time.

Nowadays things do not happen in quite the same way. Naturally, the influence of a strong man is, and always must be, felt. But outside of this there is a great tendency not to follow a leader quite as blindly as in the past. Men require something of a reason; they want an excuse for unquestioning obedience. They feel the need of answering for their acts to a conscience. In other words, there is a growing tendency, although it may at the beginning be small, to think independently, to act independently. And where this individuality of action is touched by the glow of a spiritual idea, one begins to feel something of this doctrine of private effort, of an inward mission. And when the tendency to mass-action, to ready-made beliefs, is still further impeded, the belief in the self-sufficiency of each man, each social unit, must be still more emphatic.

However, this trait may be obtained, not by a spontaneous evolution, not by a blind adherence to the ability of each person to develop in the highest way, but by such intelligent means and methods as will put him as nearly as possible on the highest plane that the majority of his fellow-creatures hold. This ideal equality

—far different from anything which society now possesses—will act for the interests of the race in the broadest extent. The *dictum* that all men are born free and equal is plainly true only in an academic interpretation. It certainly is not true as far as the actual facts of their careers can show. As far as one can see, there is as little actual freedom in the world as one can possibly imagine. Almost every adult, on reaching maturity, has a certain range of limitations, working much more rigorously than statutes enacted by law, which determine in what ways he must advance, stand still, or go backward; at the same time his freedom of choice, even of desire, is similarly defined. And, after all, one is most apt to think of his freedom as permission to exercise himself within the demarcations set up by his environment; or one might compare it to the freedom which a prisoner, bound hand and foot, has to contract his muscles. In spite of such freedom, he still is bound. And actually, a member of a civilized community is bound physically, mentally, spiritually. He can no more be said to have a real liberty of choice than a bird in a cage.

And so far as the question of what he is entitled to, what he has a right to, goes, there is very little more to be said. It is hard to find any natural right that really belongs to him, excepting, possibly, in some few cases, the right to die. Otherwise, every one of his so-called rights is the result of social and legal enactment, things to which he becomes entitled by virtue of his manner of subscribing to the rulings of the society in which he lives. The fact of being born in this society puts upon him the necessity of living in it, and as soon as he arrives upon the stage where the decision of affairs rests largely upon his immediate volition, he directly comes to see that his power of choice is very limited, that his faculty of private effort is generally very small, that only under the greatest difficulties may he have an inward mission. Whatever these forces may be, they occur not necessarily as spontaneous emotions, but rather as the result of friction, association, generally called environment.

By a related process of thought, one can easily realize that the whole sum of life belongs in its general classification to environment. The human being, in the first part of his existence, is much more unformed than is generally thought. The determining factors are not as parents usually consider them. A strong belief in heredity has become so general that direct effects of descent are looked for with all the confidence and sureness of settled and incontrovertible facts. The good father is supposed to have a good son, the virtuous mother is supposed to bear an equally virtuous daughter; by a seeming parity of reasoning, people know that homing pigeons will produce homing pigeons, fox terriers will bring forth their kind. Very rarely is the utter lack of similitude between the two sets of examples seen and insisted upon. The qualities of goodness and virtue are purely functional, the result of friction, social interaction, environment. The question of underlying physical structure, of the disposition of bony, muscular, and nervous tissue, is one of purely somatic, organic composition. And between the two there is the difference of natural inheritance and artificial acquirements.

When this distinction becomes a clearly understood fact, people will see that a new set of "rights" should be counted upon; not a right of objective demands, but rather that of subjective insistence. Parents may elect to gratify their affections, pride, and interest, by modifying the fluid potentialities of their offspring in the way that will bring most force, comfort, and welfare to all concerned. The doctrine of heredity, as commonly held, not only is falsely applied to human descents, but also renders the wisest and best efforts of training unnecessary and useless. For if at birth the child's bodily and mental organization is complete, if the acquired characteristics of parents are handed down to offspring, then there the matter ends. Every remarkable parent would have equally remarkable children, every deficient person would curse his descendants by a like deficiency; work, training, striving after noble ideals, would be useless and silly. There would be an end of private efforts, of an inward mission.

But matters are not so hopeless, as one, by following

closely the growth and development of the child, as he grows into youth and then into manhood, can see. His early stages are merely transitional; the time of preparation in which he changes from the microscopic mass of protoplasm, which is his form after conception, to the fully developed adult who constitutes the highest product of terrestrial evolution, is merely a phase of development. In these stages the young organism is played upon by an infinite number of influences that mould his body and mind according to their nature and kind. If the child is to be developed in the finest way, every possible influence that acts upon him should be controlled to serve the ends of development. The energies that belong to building up this range of potentialities should be of the finest quality, should have the greatest liberty of action, should be awarded the highest place in the community. The training which the child is to get should be what is essentially designed for him in his unripe condition, for it cannot be similar to that of an adult. So long as one recognizes that the child is absolutely different from the adult, not only in size, but also in every element which goes to make up the final state of maturity, one is more apt to get a true method of development, which must gradually bear the results of a higher evolution.

There is no doubt that many of the ideas and methods governing the treatment of children, what one is bound to provide for them, as well as what one may expect from them, are sadly deficient. The blame for this is to be laid not so much upon carelessness and indifference in parents and guardians (although these peculiarities exist), as upon a wrong conception of the problem. There is not enough of conviction in the minds of parents and guardians that the responsibility of their children's acts, either good or bad, rests upon their older shoulders, that the final outcome of these children's lives depends almost entirely upon the influences, the nutrition, the environment which the authority of the parents and guardians provide. The elements that are to be affected, being in an almost fluid state so far as susceptibility to change is concerned, require an unceasing care and attention. To break in upon the rule for a single week or day or hour defaces the beauty of the finished product, and leaves an opening for divergences from the best growth, that can later on be remedied, if at all, with difficulty. The bringing up of a child thus means a series of lessons in self-restraint, in watchfulness, in adherence to an ideal, for the parent even more than for the child. The child will fashion himself after the patterns that he sees; he does not grow according to some hard and fast rule that has been implanted in him before he is born.

When this is appreciated, one will immediately see that the world has a wrong idea of its children. It looks upon them as adults, but slightly different, in

INTRODUCTORY

the details of small size, deficient strength, little experience, from grown men and women. It believes that, were these details filled out and completed, the child would be the same as after the lapse of years he comes to be. And therefore, in consequence of this opinion, it provides surroundings for him that would be most fitted for a person of matured powers, who lacked strength and knowledge. The rules of conduct which result must, in the face of the child's real condition, be fundamentally false. Since he is in no way really like an adult, since his condition is—one of continuous change, it follows that he needs a special treatment and environment, which must be modelled upon a correct conception of what he really is. This would necessitate a remoulding of his relations and surroundings, an overhauling of ideas about comparative influences. So long as this is not done, we are apt to bear the penalty of thoughtlessness in unnecessarily deficient men and women, in the abuses which come from one-sided and twisted bodies and minds, in a stoppage of the evolution which goes hand in hand with the best evolution of the race. But first of all, we must see the truth, we must know exactly what children are, what their development is, and for what they are fitted. Later on it will be time enough to build up a system of positive treatment. Before construction, one must clear the ground, one must get rid of old material which is useless, which blocks the way. In the prospect of making a better future, is inspiration enough for the most prosaic mind.

We must recast our conceptions of the function and the scope of our children; we must look with unprejudiced eyes upon the part which they reasonably may be expected to play in the work of the world. We must conclude to give more and ask for less. It has been said that people in the world may be divided into three classes: Those who give little and ask for little, those who give little and ask for much, those who give much and ask for little. Into which classes the wise man should put himself may be left to the general conscience. The choice rightly made is in itself a discipline, a realization of the necessity for private efforts, for an inward mission.

CHAPTER II

FACTS IN THE COMPARATIVE DEVELOPMENT OF THE CHILD

CHILDREN, according to common views, are looked upon as adults in small. Most parents never stop to think of the possibility or likelihood of their own mature condition being any different from the condition of their little ones. This is somewhat remarkable, because the two are not, except in general ways, alike. Moreover, the whole world of animals seems to be similarly disposed so that the young require different conditions, different surroundings, different care, from the ordinary adult standard. Where the changes are very striking, as for instance, in the caterpillar, they are regarded as exceptions which bear no analogy in other creatures. There the transition from the creeping, rather plain-colored insect to the dormant, half-dead chrysalis, and then to the brilliant, fluttering butterfly, is so wonderful that even the dullest imagination is touched; for the wonder inheres not only in changed appearance, but also in changed methods of locomotion, food, general manner of life.

Caterpillars, however, are not the only creatures which show remarkable changes. The same idea holds good through all animal life, especially in the higher families. In fact, it is only in the very lowest forms that infancy and youth are alike. As a rule, animals, in proportion to the complexity of their organization and functions, mature late in life; the higher the animal, the longer, proportionally to the whole term of life, does it take to reach the full exercise of all his powers. A corollary of this is, that increasing complexity of organization and functions involves correspondingly great changes in actual physical states. This idea, although heretofore our attention has not been much called to it, is beautifully illustrated in human development. We have been in the habit of looking upon a child as a man in small, of looking upon a man as a child somewhat strengthened, with greater experience and knowledge. Outside of these factors of experience, knowledge, and strength, the child and man seem practically the same. So true is this observation that society founds its judgments accordingly, it prescribes its methods of education, of social and domestic care accordingly, it sees almost no differences outside of these adventitious ones between them.

As a matter of fact, it would be hard to find many salient factors, beyond the most fundamental laws, in which the infant and adult exactly resemble each other.

Multiply the proportions of the infant to those of the adult, and you will have a being whose large head and dwarfed lower face, whose apex-like thorax, whose short arms and legs give a grotesque appearance. The two do not breathe alike, their pulse rates are not alike, the composition of their bodies is not alike. The most ordinary analysis shows this. Fehling gives the percentage of water in a very young fœtus as ninety-seven and five-tenths per cent. This proportion, instead of being a permanent feature, is merely a transitory one. It diminishes steadily until, after birth, it is seventy-four and seven-tenths per cent. The decrease continues regularly, but more slowly, until in the adult it is only fifty-eight and five-tenths per cent. Even the common differences that are characteristic of various ages, and with which every one is familiar, have their foundations in actual differences of conformation. For instance, one may say that children are more supple than adults, but not merely because they are younger; it is rather because they have relatively a greater proportion of muscle tissue, and a smaller proportion of tendon. Thus there is actually less of the elements which make the body rigid. This change produces just as real an alteration in the physical being of the person as the loss of the prehensible power of the great toe, the clinging faculty, and the sucking reflex, which fade away with the passage of infancy. Again, the common necessity of eating has different objects in the two ages: in the adult the repair of body waste is the only end sought; in the child, besides this, there are additional reasons, such as the supplying of greater energy than at any previous time, and also the forming of entirely new tissue, such as would be commensurate with added growth. Likewise the deprivation from food, starvation, is fatal for each in a different way; in the adult death occurs because the amount of food is too small to atone for the processes of disintegration; in the child the same result is reached for the same reason, plus the equally or more important one that the nervous system, on account of its unstable and unripe condition, more easily and quickly becomes exhausted.

On more minute examination, one finds greater and greater differences, until one comes to believe that we have been trying to see our children in a totally false light. It is more than a figure of speech to say that the child is father of the man; it is rather a great bound of the imagination. The child is simply a stage in a development which is unstable, which changes in as due proportion as the embryo changes into the infant. From the moment of conception till full adult life, there is one continuous change that is steady, but decreasing in rapidity in proportion to the length of time during which it has been in progress. The change is universal, the different parts of the body participating in it in varying degrees. The enumeration of some of these is so convincing as to justify examining Vierordt's table, which shows the percentage weights in the new born and the adult.[1]

Some of these variations seem small when expressed in terms of percentage weight of the whole body; but when they are stated in terms of percentage of their own weight, the result seems much different, and much greater. In this latter method one could state the increase in the heart to be from twelve to thirteen times the original size, in the liver about eleven times, in the lungs about twenty times, in the brain about four times, and so on.

Take another particular instance: To say that the

	New Born	Adult
[1] Skeleton	16.7%	15.35%
Muscles	23.4	43.09
Skin	11.3	6.30
Brain	14.34	2.37
Spinal Cord	0.20	0.067
Eyes	0.28	0.023
Salivary Glands	0.24	0.12
Thyroid Gland	0.24	0.05
Lungs	2.16	2.01
Heart	0.89	0.52
Thymus Gland	0.54	0.0086
Stomach and Intestines	2.53	2.34
Pancreas	0.12	0.15
Liver	4.39	2.77
Spleen	0.41	0.346
Suprarenal Capsules	0.31	0.014
Kidneys	0.88	0.48
Testicles	0.037	0.08

child is a man in small is just as wrong as to say that the bony skeleton is the foundation and the framework upon which are laid the softer parts which it ultimately supports. As a fact, the bones in their immaturity are moulded, are pulled into this line and that by the very muscles and tendons which they exceed so greatly in rigidity. A little thought will show this to be sufficiently natural, for the bones, as every other part of the body, are continually changing, and show material differences between their infantile and adult conditions. Their final condition, as well as their function, is so different from their changing phases of growth, that the resemblance between them is merely a general one. This is interesting enough to demand an analysis of a characteristic bone, say the tibia,[1] which in itself has a deep enough meaning to serve as the basis of a theory of development and education. It is not so much a question of small variations in body composition, as of the principle underlying these variations.

Looked at in this light, it does not require much effort to show why the infant's bones are softer and

	2 Mos.	9 Mos.	3 Yrs.	19 Yrs.	25 Yrs.
[1] Phosphate of Calcium	57.54	48.55	59.74	54.84	57.18
Carbonate of Calcium	6.02	5.79	6.00	10.82	8.95
Phosphate of Magnesium	1.03	1.00	1.34	1.26	1.70
Chloride of Sodium	0.73	1.24	0.63	0.76	0.60
Cartilaginous Substance	33.861	41.50	31.34	31.37	29.54
Fatty Matter	0.82	1.92	0.95	0.92	1.84
Organic Matter	34.68	43.42	32.29	32.29	31.36
Inorganic Matter	65.32	56.36	67.71	67.71	68.42

more vascular than the adult's, nor the ultimate import of the change. One's attention is immediately turned to the idea of a consistent course of development. The difference, however, is not greater than what one sees in the marrow. This in the young is, in the first place, quite different in color from the adult form, being a fairly bright red; this is caused by the great number of dilated blood-vessels. Also it is softer and holds a larger percentage of water. It is only by slow degrees that this marrow is changed into the yellow, fatty substance which it afterwards comes to be. If one saw in an adult the condition that is regularly seen in a child, one would certainly pronounce it pathological. If we take the item of cartilage, as another particular instance, one finds that the variations still continue.[1]

Again, the infantile muscles are noticeably different from the adult, in that they contain a greater percentage of water, and a smaller percentage of myosin, as well as extractives, fat, and inorganic ingredients. Also, in the fœtal blood the specific gravity is somewhat lower than in the adult, and the specific gravity of the serum is markedly lower. On the other hand, in a few weeks there is so much change here that the specific gravity of the infant's blood is commonly higher than an adult's. The red corpuscles are in the infant poorer in hæmoglobin, as seventy-six and

[1] In the child of six months the proportion of mineral salts in cartilage is 2.24 %. At three years it is 3 %, at nineteen it is 7.29 %.

eight-tenths is to one hundred while the stroma is richer. Again, the amount of fibrinogen is relatively small, as two is to seven. The amount of sodium in solution is larger and the potassium smaller. There is a lessened tendency to coagulation. In early fœtal life the red corpuscles are nucleated, and do not attain their normal condition until after birth. Moreover, they are greater in number. Likewise is the infant's blood richer in white corpuscles than the adult's; it is richer in the so-called young-form elements, while the "over-ripe" elements are only half as many. These white corpuscles remain relatively longer in the "unripe" condition than in adults, while the latter show a larger percentage of the "over-ripe." In short, the blood of the new-born child is so clearly different from its later form, that Gundobin calls it, according to the ordinary standard of morphology, pathological. The difference in degree is so marked as to amount almost to a difference in kind. Finally, the weight of the infant's blood is relatively smaller than that of the adult's.

During the whole course of growth there are the constant factors of variation, of irregularity. These point indubitably to the fact that infancy and childhood are solely times of preparation, that in themselves they have no fixed status. And experience shows that this condition of change is easily affected one way or another. As an example, one may take the methods of development which may clearly be seen in the long bones. These consist of a narrow body, with an enlargement at each end. In the bones of the forearm and upper arm the ends removed from the elbow show much more growth than those which go to form the joint, while in the lower extremity, the parts removed from the knee grow least. Where an untoward nutrition causes a variation from the natural development, consequent changes may occur directly or indirectly throughout the organism. The changes in relations in parts such as these joints are, in some cases, exceedingly interesting. An example may be seen in the capsule of the knee joint, which in early childhood extends for only a short distance along the bone; with increased age the capsule grows more than its proportionate degree, and so extends to a relatively higher position. This difference is so great that it influences the course of certain diseases, especially where fluids seek an outlet from the joint. There is no gradual and equable growth in all parts at the same time. Both rate and location of increase are unstable. What is more, in certain parts the adult condition and shape are only hinted at in early life, and for years maintain essential differences. In such cases the purely provisional character of young growth-forms is so evident, that all doubt about their unstable equilibrium is set at rest.

We may take the growth of the mastoid bone as

an example. The external petro-squamous suture[1] does not become obliterated until the end of the first year. Then for the first time the mastoid process becomes distinct. There is, naturally, a constant formation of new bone from the periosteum surrounding it; this is accomplished the more rapidly because this periosteum, as well as that of all the body, is less stable in infants, is looser, softer, and more vascular than in adults. Thus the walls of the cavity of this bone continuously become thicker. Even here the growth is not absolutely regular, and on the average, the walls will grow from one millimetre at birth to one centimetre at nine or ten years. This new bone is fine cancellous tissue, which at puberty begins to undergo a process of absorption in scattered spots. Absorption goes on gradually but surely until these areas are thus changed into a number of connecting air cells, eventually lined by a delicate mucous membrane.

The same feature of irregularity is seen in the union of the bones of the head: while the fontanelles or inter-membranous spaces at the angles of the parietal bones normally disappear before the age of four years, nevertheless the occipital and sphenoid bones are not united at their basilar parts until the twentieth. Thus one naturally looks for a greater or less persistence of fœtal conditions, which are then seen to disappear

[1] The line of junction between the petrous and squamous portions of the temporal bone (in the head).

only gradually with increasing age. The persistence of these conditions is exceedingly interesting, and proves the wide distinction existing between infant and adult forms. In the roof of the middle ear or *tympanum* in infancy, one finds a petro-squamous suture that permits a close connection between the blood-vessels of the brain and the middle ear. This connection gradually disappears with age, but before it comes about, inflammations are with comparative frequency transmitted from the lining membrane to the *dura mater*, the tougher of the membranes surrounding the brain. The existence of such special development forms has an important practical bearing, so that the physician, when treating children, has a different problem before him than when treating adults. Another instance of gradual development is in the *foramen cæcum*, a notch in the frontal bone, which usually remains patent until or after puberty. A corresponding fact is the late appearance of the frontal and sphenoidal sinuses in the skull, which although they appear about the second and third years respectively, do not attain completion until after puberty.

Another instance of incomplete development in early life is in the orbital plate of the frontal bone, which commonly does not attain its full form until after puberty. The change in the dimensions of the orbit shows clearly the irregular growth; for while in the adult it barely equals one-third of the face in height, it makes at birth nearly one-half of it. This means that the length of the face and head in the young child is relatively smaller than in the adult. A similar rule cannot be made for the circumference, for even in early childhood this measurement is almost equal to that of the adult. The lack of proportion between the different dimensions of the face at various times is thus made clearly apparent, and the purely provisional nature of youthful forms is thus very clear. The upper and lower jaws also are very interesting, on account of their lack in infancy of permanent proportions. They begin to ossify early in fœtal life, and keep on developing and changing all through the years of childhood, until after puberty, when the final formation gradually makes itself evident. The upper jaw is really the most important part of the face, and at the same time it is the part which, naturally enough, is least developed at birth; therefore it undergoes the most salient changes before it comes to rest. As every one knows, changes in one part necessitate changes in all related parts, so that there is no one portion that one may look upon as really stable. Again, one may take as an example the layer of cartilage which acts like a cushion between those important parts of the skull, the basi-occipital and the basi-sphenoidal bones; this substance does not allow them to unite until after the twentieth year. Thus their final condition is essentially different from what it was in the preceding years. Also, in early life one finds such a disturbance in relations going on that the posterior border of the vomer[1] changes from its very oblique direction, until it becomes almost horizontal.

These disturbances serve to alter the entire shape of the head, as one can see by a few measurements. In the infant the breadth of the skull in its thickest diameter equals or even may exceed the total height of the skull and face, while in the adult it is about three-quarters of it. Again, the breadth measured between the outside surfaces of the cheek bones or *zygomata* is to the height of the face in the adult as nine is to eight, while in the infant it is about as ten is to four. Or one may look at the cranium and face, which in the adult bear the relation of two to one, but in the infant that of eight to one. This downward growth of the face is very characteristic and very important, especially when thought of in regard to its influence on the rest of the head and the neck. Originally the base of the skull is nearly flat. From this there come the rise of the basilar process in front of the *foramen magnum*,[2] the angle thus formed with the body of the sphenoid bone, and the rapid descent of the vomer. Also one finds at first the squamous portion of the temporal bone to be relatively small as com-

---

[1] A thin, irregular bone situated between the two nasal fossi.

[2] The large opening in the lower surface of the skull which transmits the spinal cord.

pared with the parietal. Some years later we find that this squamous part has increased in size more than the parietal, and also has altered its plane so as to be more nearly vertical. Besides, it extends upwards on the outer surface of the squamous portion so as to overlap it. Before these changes have been made the nasal cavity is shallow and relatively long, the posterior nares are small, and the vomer approaches the horizontal. Thus the cavity of the mouth and posterior nares is very small, because the junction of nose and throat or nasopharynx has very little height, and the perpendicular portion or ramus of the jaw is very oblique. At the same time, strangely enough, this lack of height goes together with another lack of proportion, for the distance from the back of the hard palate to the soft parts of the pharynx (excluding the tonsils) is about as great, actually, as in the adult. The change in all these details is really marked, and if one takes them separately, one can plainly see it. For instance: the lower border of the nasal opening is at birth very little below the lowest point of the orbit, while in the adult the two planes are so far apart that one would not group them together.

Such details as these, taken by themselves, may not be very interesting; but when one looks at them in the whole, they help to form a general idea that is of the greatest value. Without them the characteristic features of infancy and childhood carry with them no particular meaning. With them arranged in an orderly fashion, a plan of growth and development immediately becomes apparent. By means of such a plan, the needs of a proper environment stand out clearly and plainly — much more so than they otherwise could. Besides, an increasing knowledge of the various facts mentioned in this chapter takes on an ever-enlarging interest that grows with the thoroughness of one's information.

In the eye one finds about two-thirds of the growth accomplished in earliest infancy. On the other hand, the *recessus opticus*,[1] a transverse groove leading to the optic nerve, is more marked at birth than in adult life. But most of all, the *macula lutea*, the centre of vision in the retina, is developed only after birth. The newborn child is not prepared to see, and for some time afterwards, as sight comes to him, he sees but dimly. This is on a par with the unripe condition of the lachrymal glands, which for some weeks (and in some cases for months) secrete no tears at all. One should keep these things in mind, for their bearing upon the right exercise of the child's function of sight is of great importance. With this knowledge one would never make the mistake of expecting from a child the normally fine visual relations of an adult. The ear in its several parts, after an analogous fashion, develops very unevenly. The structures of the internal ear, the tympanic cavity, and the auditory ossicles are fairly well formed shortly after

[1] Described in 1872.

birth; but while this is true enough, the external auditory opening or meatus, the Eustachian tube, and the portion of the temporal bone behind the ear, undergo many modifications. Soon after birth the bony ring of the external ear or *annulus tympanicus* begins to grow outwards to form the floor and anterior wall of the external auditory meatus, and forwards and inwards along the outer wall of the tympanum, reaching also a short distance in the outer wall of the Eustachian tube. At this time the meatus passes inwards and downwards, and the drum of the ear or *membrana tympani* is almost horizontal.

In the ear, as well as in many other — if not all other — parts of the body, one can see in childhood the utter lack of permanent form. When the parts of an organ are not only out of proportion, but also are fœtal, and even primitive in their form, one comes to realize that human development is an exceedingly gradual process. As an example, one may cite the *tragus*, the prominence in front of the external opening of the ear. This part is commonly conical in childhood, a condition that very frequently exists before birth; and likewise it occurs as often in lower orders of the anthropoid family, such as apes.

The gradual nature of growth is well shown in the development of the passage leading from the throat to the ear, the Eustachian tube. This in the fœtus has its nasal opening below the level of the hard palate; at birth the two are on a level, while in the adult the opening is considerably higher. At birth the tube is about horizontal, but in the adult it has changed so much that its course is distinctly downward. In infancy this tube, just as we would expect, is shorter than in the adult, but at the same time it is not only relatively, but also absolutely wider at its narrowest part than in the adult. Not only is this of theoretic interest, but also, as such facts generally possess, it has an important utilitarian relation. A practical proof of this we see in the facility with which catarrhal affections of the nose and throat in the very young travel to the middle ear. In the course of development the length of the Eustachian tube doubles, but the tympanic orifice does not change its size. In short, the Eustachian tube changes in length, in size of lumen or diameter, in direction, and in the condition of its walls, but the changes are uneven and irregular; so that it and the immediately adjacent parts cannot be said to be in perfect working order until a stable, in other words, a fairly mature, condition exists.

At this early age the inferior turbinated, a thin, curled bone on the outer wall of the nasal fossa, projects slightly into the cavity of the nose; and yet, strangely enough, there is only a very minute expansion below it, and none leading up behind it. This part in these directions shows the greatest growth. It begins to increase in height directly after birth, and goes on rather rapidly till the beginning of dentition, from which time until the third year it is slow. After the first set of teeth is cut, the growth is rapid till the end of the seventh year. The increase in breadth occurs in the last-mentioned period, which also is the time when the growth of the olfactory portion is most marked. The height does not gain predominance till adult age. In adolescence the growth of the respiratory portion takes place chiefly in the middle meatus. In infancy the posterior border of the vomer is very oblique; and with the downward growth of the jaw, this obliquity is much diminished at the age of seven or eight years. Here again we see a series of changes going on, the very existence of which means not only a change in organism, but also a corresponding change in functional life, and we are not apt to recognize how remarkable these changes are, simply because they are so gradual. It is easy enough to bring up other examples where the varying conditions seem more strikingly different. For instance, in the human fœtus, at the sixth week harelip is a regular and healthy character. In later life it is a malformation.

The development of the teeth is very interesting, and at the same time demonstrative of the plainly provisional and transitional character of the early years of life. Even as soon as the seventh month of fœtal life, the alveolar processes contain a series of crypts, corresponding to the twenty milk teeth, for which they later on furnish lodgment. Soon the crowns of all these teeth are partially calcified. In addition to the milk teeth, the jaws contain the dental sacs of the permanent incisors, canines, biscupids, and first molars. The first upper molars lie behind the second temporary molars, but are not lodged in alveoli or sockets; indeed, at this period of life the crypts for the second temporary molars have no posterior walls, and so resemble mere depressions rather than clearly cut pockets. In the lower jaw the crypts for the second temporary molars extend as far back as the bases of the coronoid processes, the very top of the vertical part of the lower jaw, while the first permanent molars lie underneath these processes. Thus, at the end of fœtal life, not only are there no independent crypts for the first permanent molars, but also there is no room in the alveolar arches for these teeth, so that in the upper jaw they are placed behind its tuberosity,[1] and in the lower one are imbedded in the base of the ascending ramus. Thus one sees that the development of the permanent teeth, except the second and third molars, begins early in fœtal life, and continues for some years. The germs of the second molars appear a little before the end of the first year, but those of the third molars as late as the fifth year. As if to

---

[1] A rounded eminence near the angle formed by the lower and posterior surfaces of the upper jaw bone.

emphasize the resemblance between our children and a lower form of life, a fourth molar is sometimes found developing with, or shortly after, the other three. This occurs generally, if not regularly, among the platyrhine apes. Naturally, all these teeth undergo considerable developmental changes before their irruption, so that their final is quite different from their early states. An interesting fact is that there is not room in the young jaws for the teeth, before their irruption, to lie in a series; for this reason the central incisors overlap the lateral ones, and the canines are pushed up above the other teeth. The elements of the mature organism are stored up, and come forth little by little as their corresponding functions are brought into being and action. This idea is of universal application, and holds good not only for the teeth, but also for the entire body.

While all these changes are going on in the mouth, the tongue, in its development, is keeping an equal pace. Its shape and direction in part are not like the adult. It is greatly wanting in vertical thickness, and is long and low. Thus the soft palate rests like a curtain upon it, and when the mouth is closed, runs in the main backward, descending very much less than in the adult. This arrangement, as one can easily see, while helpful in the infantile method of feeding, would be of no use to the adult; its nature is therefore special. And one might make the same statement concerning almost every part of the young child's body. It is simply another illustration of the differentiation of function, and the corresponding changes that must go with it. Again, at the first period of life one finds the *uvula*, the pendant, soft lobe in the middle of the posterior border of the soft palate, not merely small but really rudimentary. The follicles at the back of the tongue in a similar way are very often, instead of being merely small, entirely absent. The pharyngeal tonsil is likewise rudimentary; gradually it appears and grows steadily, although slowly. Its rate of increase is so small that it contrasts strongly with that of some neighboring parts.

At the earliest stages the glands in this region, a part of whose duty is to secrete the starch-changing ferment, ptyalin, are entirely inactive, and the sugar-forming ferment practically does not for some months exist. Even afterwards its potency is noticeably small. The character of its work is almost experimental, tentative. All through this period the evidences of unequal growth are so marked that one is not surprised at examples of arrested growth, or even of change in the opposite direction. An instance of this retrograde development may be found in the thymus gland, that curiosity of the lower part of the throat, which is large at birth, in fact almost as large as the left lung, and continues to grow until the third year; then the growth ceases, and the organ remains very much, if not entirely, unchanged until near puberty, when it begins gradually to fade away or be replaced by a mass of fat. In early childhood it is so relatively large that it lies in both thorax and neck. It extends down the anterior mediastinum (the central portion of the cavity of the thorax) lies in two long lobes on the pericardium, in the membrane surrounding the heart, and by its size, keeps apart the lungs and pleuræ much more than in adults. Its development is curious on account of the large size at birth, the temporary growth, the gradual atrophy, and a certain unevenness in its disappearing, by which it fades first from the neck, then from in front of the heart, and last of all, from the first segment of the sternum or breast bone. A neighboring gland, the thyroid, upholds the general rule of eccentric growth by having its largest relative size in childhood.

Coming to the neck one finds considerable change, which, as in other parts of the body, goes on steadily, but irregularly. Between infancy and adult life the larynx sinks, as shown by its relation to the vertebral column, for a distance which is equal to about two vertebræ and two intervertebral discs. Outside of the question of absolute size, there is a real difference in relative positions. The top of the epiglottis moves from about the level of the lower border of the atlas, the first vertebra of the spine, to the middle of the third cervical vertebra, and sometimes lower. Continuing down the trachea, or wind-pipe, one finds the changes still going on, but not in the same degree; for the bifurcation of the trachea in the newly born is generally opposite the third dorsal vertebra, but in the adult it is about one vertebra lower. The top of the sternum is placed higher in the infant than in the adult, and it is relatively much smaller, especially those of males. The only exception to this is the case of some females, occasionally seen, who in this respect, as in many others, approach closely to the infantile type. This resemblance which makes itself evident in the characteristic working and the color of the lungs, as well as in other viscera, is very interesting, and carries with it conclusions that have an important bearing in matters of general life. Joining the sternum are the ribs, but in shapes that vary with the passing years. Each small epoch shows a change from the preceding time that should be regarded as a step in the progress which leads to the full evolution of the matured person. In infant life the third and fourth costal cartilages pass horizontally inwards to the sternum, instead of, as later on, sloping upwards. Likewise the lower three true costal cartilages have a more horizontal course, and the angle which these cartilages form (thus making the boundary of the anterior wall of the thorax) is much greater in the young. The clavicles, or collarbones, likewise are different, being horizontal in the very young, but inclined upward in adults.

In all this development the proportions of the chest change markedly; the transverse diameter increases more rapidly than the antero-posterior, since at first they stand in the relation to each other of one to two, while in the fully grown they are to each other as one is to three. This and other measurements in the same region help one to understand how the child's thorax should have the shape of a blunt right cone as contrary to the adult form of reversed cone. A fair idea of the change in proportions may be obtained from the fact that in the infant the upper edge of the sternum is generally on a level with the middle of the second dorsal vertebra; but in spite of the general growth, its relative position is so much altered, that before development is completed, it sinks nearly to the upper edge of the third dorsal vertebra. All in all, one may say that the ribs in early life are less oblique, are flatter and less looped up than in adult age, while at the same time the intercostal muscles, until about puberty, exert very little power over them. This accounts for the barrel shape of the young child's chest, as well as for his abdominal method of breathing, with which every one is familiar. Thus one sees that at various times there are various conditions of actual form; this implies a modified method of characteristic working, with a consequent change in the conclusions founded upon normal function.

The changes in the heart are likewise quite noteworthy. In the fœtal stages it occupies almost all of the thoracic cavity, and comparatively is much larger than at any later period. At birth it is still relatively larger than in the adult, so much so, that calculations show the newly born heart to be eighty-nine hundredths of one per cent of the body weight, while the adult heart is only fifty-two hundredths of one per cent. Likewise are the dimensions different, for on account of the narrowness of the chest from side to side, and since the vertical extent of the heart, in relation to the anterior chest-wall, is almost similar in infants and adults, it follows that the transverse diameter is greater in the child. This brings the apex beat much nearer to the mammary line, or outside of it, which is quite different from what one sees in full-grown persons. As a result, the left lung, having a differently shaped cavity to lie in than in later years, is altered in form and changed in position. At the same time, it is higher placed in children, but so curious are its relations to the chest walls at this time of life, that these are found not to be relatively low, but, on the contrary, are, when compared to fixed points in the spine, relatively high. Thus one can easily see that the whole condition is anomalous. The containing space, the relative and absolute positions, the outline and the form of the youthful heart, are quite different from what they are in later life. Also the *conus arteriosus*, the rounded upward prolongation of the right ventricle, is found to lie closer to the chest wall than in the adult, so that from the consequent friction, an opaque white patch, called the "milk spot," is often found.

The whole course of the cardiac development is irregular, so that one can find no continuous proportional rate between its growth and that of the other viscera, such as the liver, the lungs, the spleen. This does not at all agree with *a priori* expectations, for one would naturally look for an equal rate and manner of change throughout the whole body. One can merely make a very general statement, such as, that the size of the heart in childhood is relatively greater than that of the lungs, or that while the heart doubles its size, the liver increases only one-half of its volume. But such statements, if only because they are general, are unsatisfactory as far as the view of a regular and progressive organic growth is concerned. In addition, it is easy to see in the early part of life the very unripe condition of the heart, if only from the fact that there is very little difference in strength or appearance between the right and left ventricles, while, later on, the contrary is the fact. And when one is familiar with the tenacity with which fœtal and infantile conditions persist, one is not at all surprised by this, or by the common occurrence at birth of an open *foramen ovale*, a fœtal communication between the two auricles of the heart, a purely prenatal state. In fact, the farther one progresses in the study of organic development, the more is one impressed with the uneven, the unstable, the purely provisional nature of childhood.

CHAPTER III

Facts in the Comparative Development of the Child (*Continued*)

The changes in the liver are just as marked as those in the heart. During the second month of fœtal life, the liver reaches a relatively enormous size; in the third month, the continuation of this growth brings it far into the hypogastric region, and fills the greater part of the abdominal cavity. Through the rest of fœtal life, as well as in infancy and childhood, this organ is far greater in size relatively than it later on comes to be. It gradually, in proportion to the rest of the body, becomes smaller and smaller, so that from constituting one-eighteenth of the body weight at birth, it comes to be only one thirty-sixth in the adult. This in itself is sufficiently noteworthy, but looked at in the light of frequent eccentric variations in size, it loses much of its claim to a regular and normal evolution. All that one can say is, that there is a striking difference between the infant and the adult. In the latter the liver ought not to extend beyond the free border of the ribs, and is distinctly confined to the right side of the thorax, while in the former it is pushed down one to two centimetres below the free border of the ribs, and sometimes farther, and it may even invade the left thoracic region as far as to displace both lungs and heart to a considerable extent. In some cases, though without disease, it may grow to a remarkable extent, even so far as to fill up a fair portion of the abdominal space. Likewise, microscopically, there is a tardiness in complete growth, as shown by the arrangement of the liver cells, that is remarkable.

In fœtal life there are two main sorts of these cells: one is a polyhedral form, much like those of the adult organ; the other is a small round cell that gradually disappears with the lapse of time after birth. This is probably a young stage of the regular liver cell. However, it is not for some time after birth that the hepatic cylinders assume the adult mammalian type. Gradually they become longer and narrower, not so much by a change in the size of the cells themselves, as by a rearrangement of them, so that a cross-section of the cylinder shows the number of the cells to be gradually reduced to two. The gall bladder also changes its relations, for its fundus or base is farther from the anterior wall in children than in adults. The full importance of this cannot be rightly appreciated unless one gives it the dignity of a deviation from an adult normal type; and extended observation shows widely different states in the whole hepatic system in different ages. In spite of the late arrival of maturity in most parts of the body, this system seems to follow a rule of its own. Instead of showing a slow increase in absolute size, and a stationary relative condition, it exhibits a decreased relative size, and an eccentric absolute bulk. Taking up the matter of its characteristic function, the secretion of the gall bladder, the so-called bile, one sees the workings of an individual rule. For this fluid appears exceedingly early, and has even been found as soon as the third or fourth month of fœtal life. Besides all this, it also is comparatively more profuse than its adult analogue, and is thinner in consistency. Going from this noteworthy system, to a neighboring organ, one finds that the spleen is no exception to the rule of eccentric development. It occupies much the same position in both the beginning and the completed growth, but early in life it is so small as to be barely perceptible to the examining fingers. Indeed, it is relatively as well as actually smaller in children than in grown persons, and is likewise very inactive. But on the whole, so little of its actual functions is known, that one is not justified in making full conclusions concerning its development.

While, during the first period of life, the heart in its growth bears very little relation to the developing liver, it holds just as little to the lungs; for while the heart is increasing to one-fifth of its original size, the lungs take a stride that augments their growth by five-sevenths of the original volume. And from the second to the fourteenth year these organs do not come into any closer relationship. This connection, expressed graphically, seems decidedly eccentric, for in infancy the heart is to the lungs as one is to three and a half or four. Then the relatively greater growth of the lungs up to the time of puberty changes this relation so that they stand as one to seven and three tenths. At this time the growth of the heart accelerates very noticeably, so that shortly after puberty has been established, the proportion between the two organs covers the range of one to five and five-tenths up to one to six and one-tenth. On the other hand, there is a very general (but only general) relation that does not exist in childhood, for the approximate growth of the lungs resembles that of the liver, while the heart develops in a comparatively similar way to the kidneys.

One naturally would suppose that the relation between the heart and the arterial system [and arterial system] is and ought to be a close one; forming parts of the general circulatory system, one would think them so intimately connected that changes in one would necessitate changes in the other. In spite of this, however, their relative proportions undergo material changes. In childhood, in relation to the body length, one finds a proportionally small heart and a wide arterial system; but by the time of puberty these stand in the relation of a large heart and a narrow arterial system. During this time the first mentioned increases twelve times its original size, while the latter, in the same period, increases to only three times its first proportions. One may put the matter in a more graphic light, by stating that in infancy the relation of the volume of the heart to the width of the ascending aorta is as twenty-five to twenty, before puberty as one hundred and forty to fifty-six, and after puberty as two hundred and ninety to sixty-one. An associated fact is the resulting differences in blood pressure, for the conditions in early life make for a low tension, which is clearly seen in the behavior of the abdominal viscera; while at and after puberty one finds this tension much higher. Naturally, such facts as these, taken in their broadest significance, have much more of a meaning than is contained in a numerical equation. Indissolubly connected with this are problems of blood supply, excretion and secretion, tissue change, and nutrition in general. Therefore, variations in blood pressure are of the greatest interest to the body at large, and all its functions. At the same time the anomalous condition of local differences in this respect may be seen; for while the blood pressure in the body as a whole is low, that in the lungs is high. This is partly caused by the changing relations of the pulmonary artery and aorta, which in childhood bear the relation to each other of forty to forty-six, while at full development it is changed to the proportion of thirty-five and nine-tenths to thirty-six and two-tenths. The result is a heightened carbonic dioxide excretion, and a more rapid respiration in the earlier condition, and with this goes a greater nitrogen percentage. Without these conditions the naturally great activity of children would be dangerous or impossible, and they would be unable to fulfil one of the conditions of growth. Another instance of uneven local development is in the abdominal aorta and the common iliac arteries, which in the first few days are greater than at any time for the succeeding three months. Such differences right themselves slowly; but even after they have become righted, the general organism requires some time before it is accustomed to the change.

In the lungs, during the first two years of life, the walls of the *alveoli* or air spaces are thick, and their blood-vessels are loosely held. It is not until the fourth or fifth year that the proportionate adult development between the alveoli and the bronchi begins to be obtained, and the stroma or connective tissue frame-work has become dense and binding, restraining the capillaries as in adult life. Nevertheless, in spite of the approximation towards adult proportions, the neighboring parts do not immediately fall into line. This we see from the fact that the diaphragm, situated just below these structures, lies higher than in the adult. In infant life, the underlying loose tissue lining the bronchial tubes gradually and slowly binds the mucous membrane to the fibro-muscular wall. From this time it keeps pace in its growth with the other compact tissues, until in adult life it appears as dense fibrous bands. Proportionally the extent of bronchial tubes is greater than that of the air spaces, and so presents quite a different picture from what may be seen in adult life. The connective tissue of the parts is likewise more abundant and tends to a proliferation of its cellular elements. The sub-mucous connective tissue of the bronchi is loose, and more abundantly supplied with nuclei, and its vessels are less loosely held. The cells lining the air spaces form a continuous layer. The alveoli are small, their epithelium proliferates abundantly, and the absorbents accomplish their work slowly, the blood-vessels playing a more important rôle than later on. One may judge of the gradual nature of the development in the lungs from the fact that not until seven years of age, and probably later, do they reach their full forward expansion. Even from this rapid and simple account, one must plainly see how broadly different in the matters mentioned the child is from the adult. The difference, as has been said before, is not merely one of size, but also one of form, of structure, of physical and chemical importance.

Some interesting conditions are found in the kidneys. In prenatal life they very soon become lobulated, and continue so until a fairly long period after birth, when these lobules slowly disappear and are replaced by the so-called pyramids of Malpighi. The kidneys of the infant are relatively larger than those of adults, and are situated lower down. This is the more noteworthy from the fact that the lumbar part of the spine, where they are placed, is relatively small. The resulting disproportion between the parts is worthy of active attention. In the newly born child the two kidneys are equal in volume, or at all events, any difference between them is very small. During the first year this begins to change in favor of the left, and so continues to increase. At the same time this left kidney in childhood is higher placed than its fellow, and does not sink to its level until about seven or eight years of age. A curious fact is that uric acid infarctions, which are purely prenatal when found in healthy conditions, commonly exist for some time after birth. Later on in life these same infarctions would occur only in a state of pathological degeneration. The blood supply in these organs is noteworthy, for here some remarkable conditions are to be found, which weightily influence the health of the child's mind and body.

One would suppose that the growth of an organ would progress equally with its blood supply, for between them there must exist a relation almost as strenuous as that of supply and demand. But in the kidneys this is found not to hold good. In fact, it has been ascertained that the transverse section of the former increases more rapidly than the volume and weight of the latter, and the arterial tension, which depends upon the ease with which the blood is able to flow through the fine capillaries, is thereby influenced. For this reason one finds that children are more liable to renal congestion and other inflammatory conditions of the kidneys than adults, and this fact is supported by experimental researches, which prove that a greater proportional amount of water can in a given time be forced through the adult than the immature organs. In a somewhat similar degree the femoral artery increases, while, on the other hand, the common carotid, which in so large a measure nourishes the upper extremity, follows an opposite rule, having relatively an exceedingly small and slow growth. Here again purely experimental facts have the closest connection with questions of practical education and development. A very striking instance of irregularity in development is found in the suprarenal capsules; for they at birth are as large as, if not larger than, the same structures in adults. Thus time and time again the evidences of uneven development are multiplied, and what is true of the body at one time, may at another be totally false. When one considers that the average growth in body weight between birth and adult life is about nineteen times the original quantity, this stationary condition of the suprarenal capsules is noteworthy.

The stomach in its development shows some marked differences; its growth is very rapid at first, but afterwards it progresses more slowly. In infancy it is more tubular, its position is more vertical than in the adult, and the œsophageal sphincter is less developed. So real is this that the act of vomiting in young children is not attended with nearly the same amount of effort and retching as in older persons. Indeed, this act occurs with all the ease with which the contents of a bag are squeezed out. This facility is aided by the slightly higher relative position which the organ holds. In short, the evidences of immaturity, both in the gross and the microscopic arrangements, persist for a long time. Even the ducts which are so necessary to its work do not attain their permanent state until full adult life, for both before and at birth, these ducts average about seven glands to each one, but after this, owing to the continued division of the ducts, the glands are progressively divided up. This goes on until at adult life only three glands go to a duct. Besides weak peristaltic powers, the functional secretions of the stomach are of a special sort in infants. These secretions in the adult seem to possess the power of dissolving cell envelopes, thus setting free the contained proteid matter. The infant is unable to do this, for its digestive powers appear to have little or no corrosive faculty. On the other hand, its ability to digest casein is proportionally far in advance of that of the adult, and this is doubtless due to the fact that the former has a larger proportion of the hydrolitic ferment, called renin, than the latter. Thus the infant has its natural food in milk, which holds a large proportion of casein and lacks all cell envelopes. In the same way we find that the pancreatic secretions are likewise variable, for the trypsin and steapsin are barely active, and the amylopsin totally inert in infants. The digestive powers in infancy and adult life differ both in degree and kind; so that if we had no other fact than this, we should be justified in building up a broad theory of differential functions and development.

During infancy and childhood the intestines grow irregularly, by fits and starts, as it were; their position varies from that of the adult, and also they are less fixed. The constriction which may be found in adults at the junction of the first and second parts is commonly absent in infants; the transverse colon is relatively low. In the large intestine, up to four months of age, the length remains quite stationary. After that time a remarkable change takes place; the upper portion begins to grow at the expense of the sigmoid flexure, which at birth is nearly one-half of the whole large intestine, while at four months it already assumes its permanent proportions. The ascending colon in children, owing to the higher position of the cæcum and the greater size of the liver, is very short. This part of the colon has more often a mesentery[1] than in the adult, and also a relatively larger portion above the cæcum is invested with peritonæum, so that the gut is here absolutely free. The cæcum alone changes its position and relations so much in the course of development that the transitional nature of childhood is clearly made apparent.

About the fourth month of fœtal life, this part of the intestines is situated near the median plane, and at a higher level than in the adult. As it grows, it passes to the right side, in front of the second part of the duodenum, and then descends into the iliac fossa. Even then it is apt to be placed high up, near the anterior superior spine of the ilium. A corresponding position is held by the sigmoid flexure, hardly any of which is found in the pelvis until this bony basin is more widely spread out by later development. Brunner's and Lieberkühn's glands, which are necessary factors in the final activity of the bowel, are only partially developed, and the solitary and agminated glands are rich in lymphoid tissue. In fact, the whole lymphatic system is remarkably well developed in early life, and the amount of lymph in circulation is greater than it later is.

The rectum, as one would expect, shows conditions

[1] A fold of the peritonæum by which a portion of the intestinal canal is attached loosely to the posterior wall of the abdomen.

somewhat similar to the main part of the large intestine. In the adult it is situated entirely within the true pelvis, and presents three curves: one in the lateral, and two in the anterior-posterior direction. On the other hand, in the infant a large part of the rectum is in the abdominal, rather than the pelvic, cavity; it is nearly straight, and occupies a more or less vertical position. Its attachments do not extend so high in children, and the reflection of the peritonæum is placed lower down. Consideration of these facts will explain the frequency of certain infantile complaints, such as the easy prolapse of the rectum, chronic constipation, and general digestive derangements.

The bladder, also, instead of being in the pelvis, is, in early life, almost entirely an abdominal organ. The uterus grows but little from its fœtal condition until puberty. Before this time the peritonæum is reflected quite over the posterior surface of the bladder, the anterior surface of which is always uncovered by this membrane in children. In this detail the difference between children and adults, while not great, is unmistakable and constant. In the rectum also the peritonæum is reflected over the upper portion, and is relatively to the adult condition lower down. The prostate gland, like the uterus, is very small in early life, weighing at seven years only thirty grains. At eighteen or twenty years it increases to two hundred and fifty grains. The urethra follows in the same plan of being comparatively small until puberty, when its growth takes a sudden bound, until the adult conditions are attained. Naturally enough, the anatomy of the perinæum varies with that of the neighboring important parts, such as the rectum and the bladder, and with the general looseness of the *fasciæ*, the sheets of connective tissue that later on have a dense consistency, at the outlet of the pelvis. The pelvis of course increases and grows very materially, so much so, that the so-called pelvic organs, which during childhood have been more or less in the abdomen, are gradually allowed to sink and find their proper places. The change is naturally seen more plainly in the female, where the broad pubic arch and the wide transverse diameter (exceeding the antero-posterior in the adult) are characteristic of the developed state. While one looks at late changes in the genito-urinary system as right and desirable, nevertheless, one should not lose sight of the fact that such changes are merely stages in the great evolution of men and women from "*Fleisch-Puppen.*"

The spine at birth is quite different from what it finally grows to be. It is broader and shorter, but at the same time the spinal cord descends lower than in the adult for about the space of one vertebra. The whole structure is very light and flexible, so that it may easily be pulled and twisted one way and another. It is without its characteristic cervical and lumbar curves, which come into being only after the pull and strain of gravity and muscular contraction are set in motion by added maturity and increasing exercise. The various parts bear a changed proportion to each other, for the cervical (which is proportionately longer in children than in adults) and lumbar regions are equal in length, while in the man they bear the relation of two to three. In fœtal life the proportion of the movable part of the spine in the neck is greater than that in the loins, which is quite the opposite of what one finds in the adult, since in the latter the neck is the less, being about one-fifth, while the loins are a little less than one-third of the column. In later childhood the lumbar part continues steadily to grow more rapidly than the cervical, until a short time after puberty, when the adult proportions begin to be seen. In childhood a thin layer of cartilage covers the upper and lower surfaces of the vertebræ, which, however, is so small as to be of little use as a cushion, especially as the rest of the bone is not as yet completely solidified. The consolidation of the bodies does not begin till about the fourth year, and goes on till after the eighth; but the epiphyseal or end plates do not form till about the seventeenth year. The coccyx, the end of the spinal column, is particularly late in its development, for it does not begin to ossify until puberty, and then slowly progresses; as a result, the third piece is not hard until after the sixteenth year, and the fourth piece until after the eighteenth.

Some of the most interesting changes may be seen in the nervous system; by these changes man develops from a low to a very high stage of intellectual complexity. But the development is obtained only through the course of a long and complex evolution, that extends over the whole period between conception and the full, active maturity of adult life. Some time since, Goltz made experiments on a dog whose cerebrum had been removed. He demonstrated the capacity of the animal to accomplish many of its bodily functions and instincts without the exercise of the higher mental faculties. Its ability to bark, to take food, to respond to salient stimuli, was remarkable. Also, Longet amputated the cerebral hemispheres of a pigeon, and kept the bird alive for eighteen days. This bird showed ability to blink the eyes and contract the iris at the approach of a light, as well as to follow the light when it was moved about; likewise it could swallow food, as well as perform the usual excretory functions. In short, these two animals, in their maimed conditions, were not much removed, so far as fulfilling the ordinary needs of physical life is concerned, from the recently born infant. In addition, an examination of the young brain would lead one to suppose this condition, and continued examination demonstrates the gradual development from a primitive condition of simplicity into a state of normal responsible intelligence.

In children the brain is large, but chemically it contains a large percentage of water; it is therefore softer than in adult life, and the specific gravity is lower. Its gray and white substances differ very little from each other in color and composition. And not only in the brain, but also in almost all the tissues, there is a marked difference in cell formation between the young and the old. The difference is not merely one of size and quantity of cells; rather is it a great distinction in the elaboration of cell matter, so that the cells of the infant are nothing more than variants of the cells of the adult. In the former one finds a relatively large nucleus and a small portion of cytoplasm (cell-contents), while in the latter the opposite is the fact. Hodge[1] not long ago summarized this as well as the differences in pigmentation, in so clear a manner that the least attention will convince one of the widely separated structures of the two organisms.

It seems to be generally agreed that the number and extent of the convolutions of the brain bear some close relation to the intellectual power of the subject. This is interesting, in view of the conditions which one finds in early life. The morphological development is very slow — so slow, in fact, that some important cells, such as Purkinje's cells in the cerebellum, have no properly

	VOL. OF NUCLEUS	NUCLEOLI OBSERVABLE IN NUCLEI	PIGMENT MUCH	PIGMENT LITTLE
[1] At birth	100%	in 53%	...	...
In old age	54.2	in 5%	67%	33%

characteristic appearance until after birth. Even then the brain has not in its essential parts really become differentiated. According to the discoveries of Binswanger, the fully formed ganglion cells are not present in the cerebrum for at least two months, and it takes until after this time, according to the authority of Sernoff, for the cerebral convolutions to develop. The mere fact that these elements begin to grow is very far from the idea that they are as yet of any use; many changes must take place before that occurs. Some of these changes may be seen by the alteration in the position of well-known landmarks; thus the Sylvian fissure, instead of being at the level of the anterior part of the squamous suture between the temporal and parietal bones (as one finds it in adults) is one-half inch above it. These parts, although their development is more or less continuous, do not attain their permanent relations until the child is nine years old. An equally important change takes place in the fissure of Rolando, which gradually alters both position and direction. These are cited merely as instances; the rule which they exemplify holds good for the rest of the cerebral structures. For seven or eight years the development in size and complexity is rapid. From that time until after puberty it is slower and then progressively gets weaker and smaller until full maturity.

The microscopic changes are just as noteworthy as the gross. We see this when we look at the fœtal

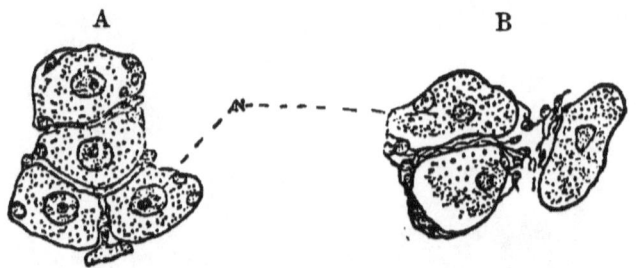

Spinal ganglion cells of a still-born male child. *N*, nuclei.

Spinal ganglion cells of a man dying at ninety-two years.

× 250 diameters.

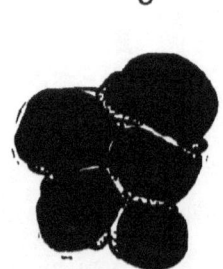

Nerve cell from the antennary ganglion of a honey bee, just emerged in the perfect form.

Nerve cells from same region (as in C) of an aged honey bee.

Showing changes in nerve cells due to age.
In the old man the cells are not large, the cytoplasm is pigmented, the nucleus is small, and the nucleolus much shrunken or absent. (Hodge.)

state, where all the cells are isolated from each other. These cells, in order to be of real use, must grow and bud and throw out branches, which later on come to interlace, like the leaves in a forest. But in the early conditions, either they have no branches, or, if they have, these branches have no connections in common, by which they are able to transmit impulses. Moreover, there is a fierce struggle for nourishment, if not for existence, among the young nerve elements, so that their initial presence does not necessarily mean their continued growth. Mistakes in nutrition, adverse circumstances of any kind, tend to make their struggle for existence harder than it naturally would be, and although attending circumstances be favorable, nevertheless the struggle must be hard. Even where they remain intact, considerable time must pass before they are able in an efficient way to carry out their peculiar functions. Thus, for instance, in the earliest time of a person's life, the conducting fibres between the undeveloped brain and the pyramidal fibres of the spinal cord perform no functions. As these fibres are the pathway by which impulses are carried from the brain to the body, it necessarily follows that the impulses are not transmitted, just in the same way and as surely that the impulses themselves cannot immediately be produced, for the simple reason that the brain does not as yet possess all of its constituent elements in a sufficiently mature condition to elaborate the characteristic functions. The inevitable conclusion is that most of a child's earliest and many of his later movements are purely reflex, not necessarily dependent upon the higher centres. For intelligent movements are merely the palpable working out of nerve tissue which is sufficiently elaborated for its peculiar functions. Fully to carry out these functions, several requirements must be met. One of these is the <u>medullation</u> of the nerve fibres. At birth the central nervous system, as well as the peripheral system, is almost entirely unmedullated. Stated otherwise, they are in an imperfect and undeveloped state. And for this reason Flechsig has pointed out distinctly that the newly born brain is "unripe."

As the child grows, each distinct advance is marked by a clear increase in the medullation. The parts, which are first able to perform their functions, first receive their myelin sheaths, so that a fairly good idea of the developing abilities of an animal may be obtained by ascertaining the extent to which medullation has progressed. As a matter of experience, we know that the purely somatic functions and reflexes exist before the higher mental qualities come into being; just as, analogously, we know that the secretion of the gall precedes that of the gastric juices, which help to break up solid food. Therefore, we find the fibres of the spinal cord, *medulla oblongata, pons varolii*, and *corpora quadrigemina* — all mainly somatic — to be

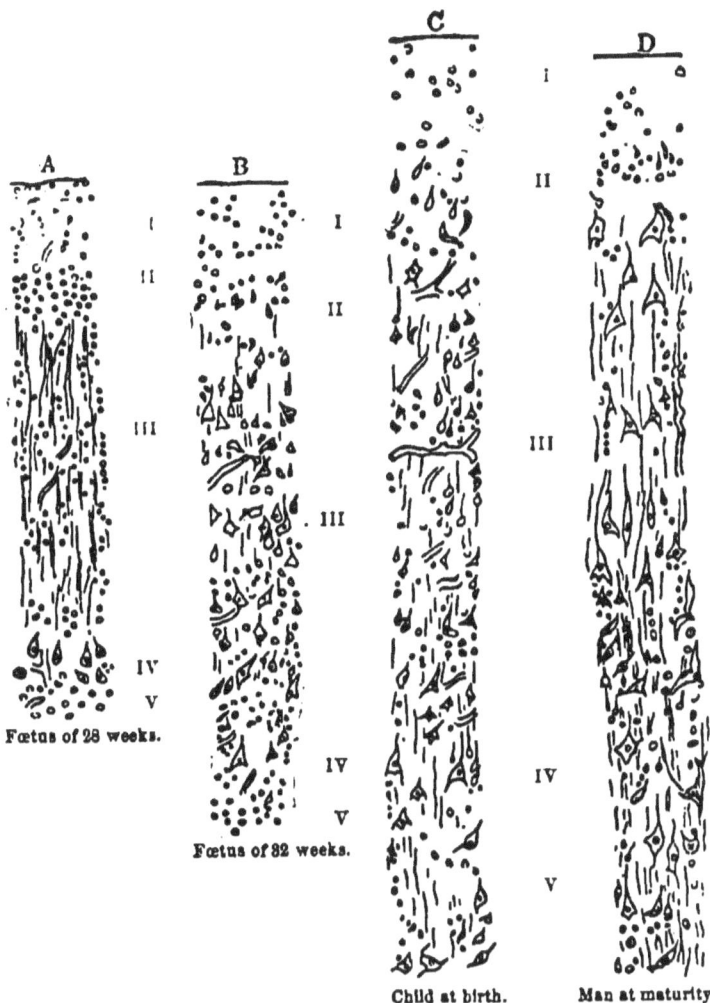

Sketch showing the increase in the number and size of the cell-bodies in the immature and mature human cortex. (After Vignal.)
I-V, layers of the cortex according to the enumeration of Meynert.

medullated long before the higher centres in the cerebrum. Likewise one can easily see the reason of all the unrestrained and objectless movements of infancy, from the fact that the inhibitory centres become "ripe" much later than the peripheral nerves. Thus the nerves whose action brings on movement are set in motion before those that restrain and control movement. The result must be an unmeasured muscular exercise that is characteristic of a low form of development. And not only the nerve fibres, but also the main and secondary branches of the nerve cells, must be medullated. This full growth occurs still later and very gradually. One can see at increasing ages the slow advance of this process, as the cells throw out their branches from year to year, at first in small separated groups, which grow and spread until they finally merge together between puberty and adult life; but it must be remembered that the process is slow, and for a long time confined to small localized areas. Likewise one must remember that even when the branching out is in process of formation, the results of its activity are tentative and unreliable.

One obtains a most convincing experience in studying the development and growth of the nerve branches. The nerve cells exist at first without them, and acquire them very slowly and gradually. First a process of cytoplasm pushes its way out more gently and tenderly than a wonderfully fine shoot grows out from a root through the surrounding soil. This process is called the neuron.[1] After a sufficient period of growth it begins to divide and subdivide, so that finally a mass of the finest shoots spreads out on both sides and in front. These are called dendrons. Now the capacity both to receive and deliver impulses is a function of these branches and their end pieces; and also they must be still further differentiated so that they may determine which shall conduct the efferent and which the afferent impulses. Thus the shape of the cell and the number of its branches have a most important bearing upon the nervous activity of the person.

In all probability the cell bodies make up less than ten per cent of the entire weight of the central system, so that the remaining ninety per cent must be made up of neurons, dendrons, and other similar tissues. In the vertebrate series the cortical cells tend to possess more branches in direct ratio to the high position which the animal occupies in the zoölogical series. The higher the animal and the more complicated and fruitful its

[1] It is obviously impossible to give a full history of cytogenesis. If one wanted to do this, one would have to delve into the complexities of dendrones and dendrites, of neurons and neurones, of axones, collaterals, telodendrites, of arkyochrome, stichochrome and gryochrome cells. Such reading is plainly for the scientist who has a fair measure of precedent knowledge in this field. The best that one can do is to refer the reader who may be anxious for further knowledge to the works of such men as His, von Leubossek, Retzius, Ramon y Cajal, Kölliker, and others like them who have done such wondrous things in this fascinating department of research.

physiological economy, the greater the number of these branches must be, and Cajal's figures show positively that each cell passes from a condition in which it has no or few off-shoots into one final state, in which it has an exceedingly great many; and that this increase grows steadily, but with progressively greater slowness, up to the time of maturity. In addition, all the medullated neurons are in their early history unmedullated, the process being completed with great deliberation. Thus, even if the medullation in the peripheral system was for the main part completed in the first seven years, nevertheless several more years would be needed before the process had spread sufficiently far in all directions to put the child on a plane approaching that of the adult. Especially does this seem true when one realizes that the main advances in the first few years are in the motor and sensory fibres, and that these fibres make up only one-third of the whole area of the cortical surface, the other two-thirds being reserved for higher uses.

Still another important factor in nerve development is the presence of chromatin granules. Unfortunately, our knowledge of these bodies is as yet limited, but nevertheless we are certain that they are closely associated with the functional activity of nerve structures, and that they are absent in the very young. As the animal increases in power and functional activity, these granules grow more and more evident.

Thus, when we see a puppy sprawling about, unable to walk after the fashion of his kind, and unable to see, we must assign the cause not necessarily to physical weakness and stupidity, but simply to the fact that the animal's nerves are not yet medullated, that as yet he does not possess the sufficient amount of chromatin granules, that as a whole his nervous system is "unripe." The same idea is true of children. They are different from adults not merely in size, stature, strength, and experience, but much more in the inefficient development of their various organs. Their helpless condition is not necessarily due to lack of strength, but rather to inability to use the strength which they possess. One should call to mind the well-known experiments of Dr. L. Robinson on sixty new-born infants. He proved that they were able to hang by their hands from a stick for thirty seconds. This is almost as remarkable a performance as walking, and involves a striking amount of strength. The reason why this strength can be used is, that the clutching and grasping faculty is one of the first somatic functions to be developed, that the nerve cells controlling this function are subject to an exceedingly early elaboration. The children, as a whole, are "unripe"; they stand in the place of the chrysalis, of the immature animal that is so far different from its fully grown model as almost to merit the name of a different **creature**.

Thus, for instance, as soon as one looks at a baby's brain, one is able immediately to see why he cannot walk like an adult, for outside of the microscopical changes, the cerebellum, where the function of coördination is seated, is relatively much smaller than the cerebrum. In addition, one sometimes finds primitive conditions in this part, which show that development must bridge over a great chasm before useful functions exist in a normal state. Thus one may mention the median occipital fossa noted by Lombroso in connection with the hypertrophy of the vermis of the cerebellum, which sometimes occurs in the very young human being. This condition regularly occurs in the lower apes. For similar reasons one would conclude that useful and reliable sight comes to the child more slowly than is commonly believed. Just as in walking the loose and unregulated movements of the legs become rarer and rarer, so the ability to see clearly, to understand the meaning of distance, to grasp the idea of the third dimension in space, has a very gradual, even slower growth. In the real sense of the term, the child for some weeks does not see at all, and for a long time he sees very imperfectly. His first distinctions are merely those of light and darkness, then the warm colors, and finally the colder ones, with their various shades. Professor Preyer, wishing to get positive information on this subject, trained his young child by daily practice in discriminating between the various colors. When the child was almost two and one-half years old, although he could pick out, with fairly good accuracy, such strongly marked hues as red, yellow, and black, nevertheless he seemed absolutely unable to distinguish green, blue, gray, and orange. And even in the fourth year he failed to recognize the difference between blue and gray. This case is all the more impressive, because the child had a special training, as well as environments, which naturally would be productive of good results. But one cannot easily abolish the limitations of nature.

In these chapters I have been forced, on account of the wealth of material, to use many isolated facts. A complete account of all the slow changes that make the child so widely different from the adult would include almost every item of physical and mental growth. There was a real necessity of picking out only enough to form the outlines of a picture. But the picture should be so plain that any one and every one may know the meaning of it. This meaning includes the clear facts that an infant's development is not a rigidly immovable process, that it progresses slowly and irregularly, and that during its course the child is in so unstable a condition that no strain should be put upon his faculties. It is easy to see that an organism which is in a condition of unstable equilibrium may, by seemingly slight causes, be injuriously affected. Where the organic elements are so delicate, where their relations are so changing, where so long a time is necessary to insure their normal and healthful completion of growth, it must be clearly evident that the artificial conditions which constitute their environment must play an important part in deciding the value of their ultimate activity. Such things, taken together, go to form a child's nutrition, for this term cannot rightly be used to designate only his food.

On the contrary, every fact which affects metabolism, tissue-change, must be included in this term, nutrition. The conservation of energy in motor impulses, sense impressions, physical exercises, comes within the boundaries of this category. The child whose sense of sight is wrongly or too early taxed, whose power of food-assimilation is abused, whose order of mental development is ignored, is suffering from poor nutrition. This child who prematurely participates in experiences and ways of living, who is allowed to wander outside of the limits that a conservative idea of growth imposes, who becomes subject to conditions that only the strength of maturity can withstand, is thus subjected to adverse conditions that must surely leave their mark upon his later organic form. Such a child is suffering from a vicious nutrition. The child who assumes responsibilities beyond his years, who undergoes the wear and tear attending the course of a too rapid development, who lacks the benefits of a wise restraint and discipline, is bound to show the effects in a partial and one-sided development that bars him out from the full beauty of finished maturity. Such a child suffers from the effects of a misdirected and vicious nutrition.

We have the word of M. de Lavelaye, a wise man in his generation, that success in life does not mean proficiency in money-making, in professional skill, or in any form of special activity. Rather it means that a man should represent the best civilization of his time, that he should stand for intellectual strength, moral strength, that he should be strong in his affections, amenable to proper authority, mindful of his natural and artificial limitations. Such a man would represent the finest flower of human life; his presence would be an inspiration and an example to all who come in contact with him. At the same time, the fact of his existence would mean that every part of him stands in absolute harmony with his whole organization. There could be no one-sidedness, no atrophy of one function associated with hypertrophy of another. Such a man would represent the workings of a system which nourished in the proper order and manner every group of cells in his body. And when his nutrition was so devised as to bring him into the best working with his environment, he would naturally attain the excellence which we now look upon as an ideal. The more one regards the facts in these two chapters as truths of fair observation, the more one is forced to feel that the ultimate condition of a child is dependent upon a law which embraces these truths along with many others in a generalization which must cover the whole range of human experience. Such a generalization, stated not too strongly, would convey the impression that a child is the creature of surrounding, modifying influences, that he is, to a large extent, what his environment makes him, that in the first place, the responsibility for his development rests heavily upon those who provide the environment.

It is always a good thing to know where one stands, to know the effects of one's acts, to know what measure of praise or blame one deserves. Thus, in so far as the mind is free, can one mark out a path along which to walk. There can be no doubt of the truth of this; and whatever truth it has applies strongly to one's relations to children. It must ever be the part of wisdom to recognize how far their true development is independent, and how far it is bound up with a knowledge of their evolution from exceedingly low forms, by means of carefully modifying circumstances, into forms of wonderful complexity and fineness.

CHAPTER IV

COMPARATIVE IMPORTANCE OF HEREDITY AND ENVIRONMENT

"LIKE to like" is a common expression; "like from like" is as commonly understood. The fact of related forms and functions usually implies a connection and similarity in origin and development. One knows from ordinary experience that roses produce roses, that horses bear horses; what is more, one expects a still further distinction; an American Beauty rose never grows from a Maréchal Neil, nor does an Hambletonian mare give birth to a Percheron. In addition still, successful attempts have been made by growers of plants and breeders of animals to control to some extent the character of the respective progeny. Following such efforts, some of the best results of intelligent application have been accomplished. By crossing roses of a particular size and color, the size and color of the offspring plant — as every one knows — may be approximately determined. And so certainly is speed in the parent horses bound to develop speed in the foals that the get of prize-winners merely upon the form of the parents command a high price.

Most people, reasoning from such ordinary facts as these, believe that children in their nature follow that of the parents, and they expect a brilliant father to have a brilliant son, just as they look for a moral-minded child from moral-minded parents. So confident is their reliance upon this rule that an exception to it provokes curious and wondering comment. A man whose parents are criminal is regularly looked upon with suspicion, just as a criminal whose parents are respectable is regarded with even more disfavor, if that is possible, than is his fellow-sinner, whose heredity is bad. Most persons go even farther than this: they expect a man's occupation or the acquired characteristics which his occupation entails, to influence his child's character. Facility in certain trades and aptitude for various professions have often enough been traced to the fact that one or both parents had acquired an experience in these vocations. Scars and mutilations in the parent commonly serve as good cause in many people's mind for the accidental occurrence of approximately similar markings in their offspring. If a clergyman has a wild son, the friends and relatives feel that the boy is a lapse from the expected order of things, a sort of freak of nature. Nevertheless, Galton, an authority in questions of heredity, believes that clear reasoning will show grounds for expecting such "freaks."

Extended observation will show that such cases of

resemblance are largely coincidences. The more consideration one gives to the matter, the more one finds exception to the common rule of expecting a man's children to be an imitation of him, or even of expecting the child to represent the sum of father and mother. In the simplest organisms, such as *protozoa*, on account of the simplicity of the elements involved, this would be the fact; for here one would have creatures practically alike and homogeneous, which have been created by the cutting in two of the parent. There would be no question of artificial circumstances, of artificial adjustment to environment, of acquired tendencies to be considered. In fact, in all the lower forms of life, the question of reproduction is less complex than in the higher. Thus one might divide a hydra into small pieces, and from any one of them a new creature could grow. Or, by planting a slip of a begonia in the ground a whole plant might be started. But as soon as one has to do with the higher order of animals, different conditions come into play; there is an added complexity of development and function, and with this added complexity come countless elements to make the equation so much harder to solve. Descent is no longer a matter of simple fission of cells, a plain reproduction of a homogeneous material. Rather it is an elaboration of many different sorts of tissue, which have the possibility of assuming the most intricate functions. Thus in man one has the most complex being, who is affected in his physical and mental constitution by countless ancestors, each one of whom has contributed a share to make up the present whole. By the very fact of his complexity of constitution and functional arrangement, he makes up a problem that is quite different from anything that lower animals offer us. In reasoning about him, one is very apt to confuse purely personal and acquired traits, that are the result of circumstance, with facts of rigid inheritance that circumstances can never alter.

There is, besides, one important factor in his descent that is almost entirely absent from the descent of all other creatures. In them there is practically a clear line of ancestors, most of which lived in the same places, in the same conditions, under the same influences. The changes that have been traced in them are slow, gradual, and directly attributable to adaptation to environment. The Indian tiger has had no opportunity to be crossed with the American jaguar, nor does the horse breed with the cow. Each kind of animal follows a general system of in-breeding that keeps its strain fairly pure and simple. Cases of commingling and inter-breeding from widely separated sources are, therefore, not common. And thus the main characteristics have been preserved with a remarkable degree of purity. In man the opposite is the case. For countless ages, as the result of victory and conquest, of migration, of travel, of curiosity, of intelligence, of many-sided necessity, he has been moving about in habitable lands, making all sorts of social, domestic and political connections, both transient and permanent, with the result that his race is a most strikingly mixed one, mixed beyond hope of picking out — among civilized peoples at least — a really pure strain. There is no class of animals, even in the remotest wood or jungle, that is so utterly tangled in its heredity. As instances of this process of mixing, one may cite some of the very interesting studies in anthropology, recently made, which have picked out the trails of wandering peoples, and their effects upon the characters of the people of the traversed localities. The deeper the study is pursued, the less can one believe in a "pure strain." The progress of the Teutons alone is most instructive. They had certain characteristics, among which were tall stature and fair complexion. All over the map, wherever these "greasy seven-foot giants" have gone, they have stamped these characteristics upon the population, so that centuries have not wiped them out.

Again, in the Armorican Peninsula there is a strongly marked contrast between the Bretons and the other French peasants, who live side by side. When the coast people are compared to those of the interior, the differences come out with great strength. This is hard to understand until one remembers that in ancient times this coast was invaded and ravaged most fiercely by the Saxon pirates. So thoroughly did these

Northern barbarians leave their impress upon the inhabitants, that even to this day the Teutonic complexion of eyes and hair, and the shape of head, in other words, purely somatic traits, still persist. In other places, types persist for thousands of years, in spite of mixing, in spite of conquest; so that in the confusion of ages, old-time traits are continually cropping up. At Dordogne, in the Limousin hills of France, a distinct type of man occurs, that is said to be a remnant of the very ancient Cro-Magnon race. It existed in prehistoric times, in ages when the inhabitants of France were below the level of the American Aborigines at the landing of Columbus, at a time when the climate was so different that the reindeer roamed over what is now the Valley of the Rhone. In spite of time, conquest and occupation of the country by foreign tribes, by the Romans, the Saracens, the Teutons, this race has in part persisted. Like outcropping strata in the earth, their characteristics have from time to time, and in various places, appeared again and again. But always, one should remember, have these characteristics belonged to the category called *somatic*. The acquired traits are entirely different, and are not in the same way transmitted. What combinations have resulted from all these admixtures, surely no one can tell.

One may find another example in the Jews. Of all peoples, they, doubtless, are the most purely bred.

They had a distinct ethnic existence for centuries before the ancestors of their modern neighbors were redeemed from barbarism. They have retained for thousands of years certain well-known features of face, form and mind, that give them an undoubted race-individuality. But, nevertheless, they bear the marks of their wanderings. They are a sort of living record of an organic process which has come down from the remote past to the present. Every people among whom they lived have left their mark upon them. The branches that lived in Russia show characteristics that are purely Slav; in others there are traits that are clearly Iberian; in others one can see signs that point with an unwavering finger to a sojourn among Teutons; mixed with the pure Semitic traits are features which point with an unerring directness to a widely foreign element. These traits are heritages from all past time, modern as well as ancient. Taken together, they make a curious mixture. But the one exists as well as the other; for to-day, in the streets of New York, one may easily recognize skulls and lineaments that are as clearly ancient Assyrian as one can possibly hope to find.

In the same way that bodily characteristics reappear for generations and centuries from a far distant source, so traits of mind and character are similarly cropping out. Such things are beyond direct control; they are the result of a complicated miscegenesis, and their existence does not in any way depend upon the efforts or the acquired characteristics of parents. They come from very many origins, and their occurrence, as well as their action upon one another, no man can predicate. Moreover, whenever a union between members of different races occurs, an indefinite number of ancestral traits appear, which seem to be set free by the very fact of cross-breeding. This effect of crossing is well known, and is illustrated by such classical examples as Darwin furnished: the mule, the offspring of the horse and the ass, frequently is born with stripes upon the legs. This feature is not seen in either parent, but is traced back to a remote ancestor of both, which was a zebra-like animal. Another instance which he cites is the case of domestic pigeons, the various breeds of which are supposed to be descended from the blue rock-pigeon. He crossed two mongrel birds whose coloring was totally unlike that of the rock, "and they produced a bird of as beautiful a blue color, with the white loins, double black wing-bar, and barred and white-edged tail-feathers, as any wild rock-pigeon." Such facts in regard to animals do not strike the general reader as especially wonderful. He has become so accustomed to hearing startling accounts of heredity in the breeding of animals, that nothing astonishes him. Apply similar reasoning to man, and the outcome will appear to be and is beyond all computation. For every child may show all manner of reversions; he may bear the mark of a remote ancestor who lived far back in the past, or he may embody a mixture of characteristics that is different from the component elements which go to form it. This is almost certain to happen, because there is no family that has for a sufficiently long time been absolutely able to control all the various unions that have occurred in its line. Most of all is this true because no person is quite of one type in all his physical and mental composition. One would think, according to the usual reasoning concerning inheritance in animals, that the most strongly marked traits, no matter what they were, would most surely leave deep impresses upon descendants, that a characteristic feature of the parent, of any sort at all, must be reproduced in the child; but this does not necessarily follow. On the contrary, one finds that the opposite often is the case. Thus one rarely sees the son of a great musician equal his father in musical ability, or the son of a great lawyer take equal rank with him. What usually happens is that the hereditary ability, if there be any, shows itself in the form of a predisposition or a tendency, which, on account of the influence of the father's prestige, is apt to be magnified beyond its real worth. Thus one sees, more and more, that the plain, simple rules which govern the descent of animals cannot apply to that of man. Our human conditions are so complex, are so clearly the result of an artificial arrangement of affairs, that the resulting combination of things is quite different from what it would be, were we living in a state of nature. The laws, customs and discipline of civilization, while fitted to conserve the general welfare of society, are not at all designed to carry out the stringent laws of heredity. The result is, that by the combination of unnumbered ancestral traits and present artificial conditions working upon each other, we can be sure of very little in conclusions regarding heredity, and must be satisfied with the seemingly indefinite and dim consensus of forces which, in a general way, we call predisposition.

The question of predisposition is a quite different one from that of strict heredity; for here, instead of absolute reproduction of form or disposition, or both, there is merely such a moulding force at work upon the child's structure that the influence of environment is enough to turn the son in approximately the same direction as the father travelled. For reproduction, all the elements in question must be represented in the parent's germinal cells. There is almost nothing to prove that what does not exist in these cells can possibly be transmitted. For instance, moral training is no more an essential part of these germinal cells than good manners, nor is a cultured taste more certain to be passed on to the next generation than a fine knowledge of the flavor of tea. The most that can be said of predisposition is that certain human beings are so constituted as to act as good growing grounds, as good culture media, for a certain sort of impulse. And when outside conditions fall in such a way that influences favorable to the growth of certain states of mind or body exist, the characteristic reaction must result. Thus a child may have a natural inclination toward morality or industry or light-heartedness; if the proper conditions exist, the quality in question will grow in commensurate degree. The "mute, inglorious Miltons" are mute and inglorious because they have the predisposition toward poetic conception and expression, but in other requirements are not sufficiently fortunate.

In a somewhat similar way people are known to have a predisposition to certain sicknesses, say tuberculosis. Very few men of scientific training now speak of consumption as an hereditary disease. Rather they say and think that the person in question is of such a constitution that he very easily, under proper conditions, becomes a fertile ground upon which the germ of tuberculosis may grow. In this way an increasing number of diseases that at one time were thought to be absolutely hereditary are now counted, rightly enough, as either cases of direct infection of the child by a definite disease-germ from the parent, or merely a liability, a predisposition, in the child to that sickness. The child before birth may in this way be attacked by small-pox, malaria, measles, scarlatina,

Asiatic cholera, or croupous pneumonia; he may be born with any one of them; but that does not say that they are hereditary diseases. All that one may with safety state is, that the germ has reached the unborn infant, and finding a fertile soil, has lived and flourished thereon. This is quite different from the idea that the connection between parent and child necessitates an unvarying transmission of an acquired disease, which, so long as it once exists, must run a definite course. There is always, in addition, the counter-fact that a predisposition of any kind may be more or less successfully combated. A fertile place may, as every one knows, be rendered less fertile, and also may be made sterile.

There are many cases where common opinion supposes a congenital condition to be the result of heredity, of undoubted transmission from parent to child of a condition that formerly was thought to be beyond the range of interference. In these instances, careful thought cannot possibly agree with the supposition. A case in point is the belief, so rigorously held, that epilepsy, in all its various phases, must be a distinct disease that is in some invariable fashion handed on from one generation to another. Some years since a successful attempt to produce epilepsy artificially was made. Obersteiner, by various operations and mutilations of the nervous system, produced an epileptic condition in guinea pigs that imitated very exactly the symptoms of the natural disorder. A somewhat similar condition consequently showed itself in the direct offspring of these animals. Ordinarily people would say that the disease was thus proved to be hereditary, that the parents suffered from it, and in due time their product showed like symptoms. On less of a basis than this many serious beliefs have rested; on even a slighter basis many mothers have founded a strong faith in the efficacy of accidental impressions made upon a child before his birth. As a matter of fact, a more logical explanation would lie in the idea that the parents, by reason of their serious mutilations, came to have weakened and irritable nervous systems, and although they could not transmit the operations which they underwent, nevertheless, their young, as far as their brains and nerves are concerned, were feebly endowed. Various sorts of nervous irritability, among which were epileptoid manifestations, inevitably resulted. It is still easier to understand the occurrence, which is often a coincidence, of the so-called maternal impressions. Many mothers during pregnancy undergo some shock or nervous strain. The greater this is, the greater is the likelihood of interference with the nutrition of the infant, not as a matter of direct inheritance, but only as a method of lowering the mother's vitality, and through it, the child's. Whatever mark or blemish is noticed after birth is very apt to be referred to some of the countless experiences in daily life to which it bears some real or fancied resemblance. So many of these experiences happen in the ordinary life of every person that there is no lack of them to serve as cause for whatever misfortunes that may occur. No notice is taken of the other countless accidents of all sorts, the vast number of disagreeable smells, sights, and sounds that assail every woman, whether pregnant or not. The innate desire to know the reason of things leads people on past the bounds of reason into the field of conjecture. This was finely and characteristically illustrated in a case that came under my notice a short time ago. A child was born with a mark on the back which in a general way represented the shape of a net. The mother then remembered that about four months previous she had accidentally been struck with a tennis ball, and lo! there was the picture of a tennis net. Examination showed the mark to be merely a nævus of an irregular and broken contour.

One must clearly understand that heredity in its action is comprehensive, far reaching, not easily moved. The individual is not, in his somatic constitution, easily affected, excepting in a theoretical sense, by slight influences of an extrinsic nature. Thinking in a purely ideal way, there is reason to believe that a certain part of the fertilized ovum, called the germ-plasm, is composed of two particles of similar matter derived from the parents, which parts, in their previous turn, had their origin from the grandparents, and so on. This germ-plasm is thus properly, so long as the race exists, immortal; it can never die so long as men beget and women conceive; it is practically unchangeable. It is accompanied by a so-called body-plasm from which the body develops. This is the part that changes with the passing months, that comes to bear the mark of external influences. The distinction between these two factors is a plain and salient one, that should, by all means, be clearly appreciated. The germ-plasm is as old as man, the body-plasm is just as old as the person to whom it belongs. The one may be called his real ancestral part, that varies merely as the resultant of the two lines of parentage conjoined. The other is his physical self, the sum of the influences of nutrition. This thing called nutrition is the main fact of interest to those who believe in training. It is the only part in man that is susceptible of cultivation. To try to cultivate anything else is much the same as trying to civilize a remote ancestor. Thus at a glance one can see that only in a partial way is development hereditary. Where somatic characteristics end, there heredity begins. A fairly important part of each person is born in a certain state without the possibility of change, and an attempt to influence it would be about as feasible as trying to bring a three-legged man into existence.

When one resolves the ordinary ideas of development into their last factors, one sees that what is usually meant by heredity is something quite different, is what should be included under the head of <u>effects of nutrition</u>. For instance, through some fault in nutrition, the process of ossification in the palate bone of a baby does not proceed far enough, the prenatal condition remains stationary, and a cleft palate is the result. Or, by an analogous factor in the nutrition of nerve cells, the developing child becomes grave or gay, brilliant or stupid. Or a father has fallen a victim of syphilis; the body-plasm of his child is so affected that it shows the mark of the disease. Here again the result is one of nutrition, and proper attention to the environment can change the condition to something quite different. Here, then, is one of the most important facts in human life: the effect and the value of environment. This is the fact which does more than anything else to make people as we see them. As a matter of essential construction, men are all very much alike, for since they must have had the same evolution, they differ from each other mostly in the results of nutrition, of environment. Germ-plasm is so little susceptible of change, is so rigid in its constitution and disposition, and has been so thoroughly subjected to inter-breeding and cross-breeding, that to mark off one man from another is wellnigh impossible.

On the other hand, the medium in which a child is

conceived, born, and nourished, is of the most telling value. His body and mind are predestined to certain conditions, not so much because he is descended from this line or that, as because certain obstacles retard him, or certain means of help carry him forward. These obstacles and helps are of no one particular sort; they are spread over the whole sum of human experience. They begin long before the child is born, they continue actively in force until maturity, they then gradually decrease in a vanishing ratio. Conventional opinion says that a child is well born if his family has won a greater measure of applause than disfavor, if he has a body that is fairly regular in its parts, if his moral nature is of a sufficiently normal type to rebel at flagrant offences against morality and the public interest, as usually understood, and if his intellectual powers are sufficient to permit his making himself understood, and enable him to support himself. Now, for almost all of these factors he is not responsible, nor are they necessarily qualities which his parents possessed, or are capable of transmitting. He comes into the world as a mass of potentialities, for months he is the most neutral of creatures, whose functions are largely reflex and automatic, whose mental vigor is really *nil*. Little by little he gathers strength, the parts of his body gradually spread out in the irregular ways of rapid growth. Measured by the standard of normal maturity, every piece of him is out of measure, is provisional, almost pathological. His whole constitution is temporary, and cannot even be regarded as the foundation of what he eventually will be. He is so plastic that his daily surroundings mould him as surely as a warm hand shapes a piece of wax. With added growth he approaches very slowly to the ordinary level; but all his movements of mind and body are marked by the clumsiness, the wavering uncertainty of an unprepared state. His weakness cries aloud for affection and care. The answer ought to be given in the fullest protection, the absolute shielding from every sort of strain, mental, moral, and physical. He is in no condition to bear burdens, it is hard enough for him to find out that there are such things. His principal work should lie in being formed, in getting a straight back, big lungs, and a clear mind; in possessing a nervous constitution which, as one of its functions, is capable of elaborating a moral sense that points straight. For such things are guaranteed by nature to no one. Moreover, the child is so easily influenced, and the number of controlling factors about him is so large, that unless there is a fixed and constant plan of action, which is designed to fashion him in a certain manner, his final condition will be settled by a ragged combination of chance influences. Under such circumstances, it is not at all wonderful that anomalous differences between parents and children commonly exist.

The problem is finally one of nutrition in the broadest sense. Whatever makes for the fullest development of cells is properly included in this term. Food, rest, tissue change, stimulation and over-stimulation are all merely parts. As the previous chapters and the plates facing pages 55 and 56 clearly show, the child is in practically every respect different from the adult, and every part of him is constantly changing. The only conclusion which one may draw from these facts is that his environment ought to be designed to further the proper growth, that his needs are different from those of his matured relatives, that disturbances of mind and body occur in him with the greatest readiness, and may produce immovable harm. These disturbances are generally due to the environment; faulty food, faulty methods of rest, faulty ideas of excitement, are some of the causes involved. And, considering the importance of the matter, it is really wonderful that greater attention has not been paid to it. A man who without a proper training attempts the conduct of a suit at law would draw down ridicule upon himself; he who without a sufficient course of instruction prescribes for the sick is punished by fine or imprisonment; even the most ordinary workman needs an acquaintance with the nature of his work, before an employer will put a task in his hands. But for the right care of children no training in the mothers, nurses, or teachers is considered essential. One of the natural results is that the standard exacted among such persons, instead of being very high, is very low. With them the main test of whether a child is being properly fed is that he does not die, the test of whether he is properly clad is that he does not freeze, the test of whether he is properly taught is that he sit quietly in school, and pass a sufficient number of examinations. As a matter of fact it would, doubtless, be better in many cases that he should die, or starve, or remain "uninstructed."

The period of childhood involves, proportionally, more work, excitement and strain, than any other part of life. The little one has to eat all manner of strange foods, to learn the meaning of all sorts of strange things, to conform to all kinds of rules of conduct that are clearly artificial, the use of which he cannot understand. One can easily understand the difficulties of becoming accustomed to such requirements, when one knows that each of these items is of prime importance. Various articles of food differ very much from each other, and in their final use serve diverse ends. A child that is growing and learning some new fact of experience every hour, whose delicate nerve cells are not able to bear any great stress, needs an exact and wise attention to his dietary, much more so than, for instance, his father. The latter can, with benefit, live upon a mixed diet, and whether he consumes a somewhat smaller or larger percentage of proteids or of carbohydrates, is a matter of comparatively little importance. His organism merely seeks to repair waste. But in the child the main object is an added one, the element of unimpaired growth. Every ounce of assimilated nourishment counts, every small bit of waste energy has its telling effect. And in the matter of growth, it is necessary to remember that each element in the body calls for its particular sort of nutriment. Brain cells require proteid matter, bone tissue requires certain mineral salts. A dietary rich in starch (as in many vegetables and cereals) would serve neither one of these tissues. The distinctions between foods may be even more finely drawn. The curd of cow's milk is hard of digestion, much more so than that of some other mammals. A child with a delicate organism that requires a milk food might starve on cow's milk, even though its quality, *per se*, be very good. Or even if he lived, he might be poorly nourished, and show the effects in a locally or generally weakened body, or in a dull or abnormal mind.

As he grows, his life experiences, in the ordinary family, broaden, far more rapidly than his development matures. The need for nourishment, for the right apportionment of the various elements of food, increases progressively. And in like measure, the danger of partial tissue-poverty increases. The faculty of emotional excitation is almost always neglected.

There is no general idea of the necessity of regulating such impulses to the end of conserving energy. Fear, sorrow, joy, shame and love, in improper measure, are broad avenues of waste. When he goes to school his work is enormously increased; school authorities seem to think that their duties are best interpreted by putting upon children the heaviest instead of the lightest possible burdens. In fact, I know of no harder experience, no more trying ordeals, than what a child at this time undergoes. His experiences in the school environment are finely designed to encourage irritation and waste of nerve and muscle tissue; the circumstances of instruction are useful for deadening instead of encouraging a normal standard of intellectual development. And it is just at this time that the diet receives the least attention. One would think that under such conditions an incentive for insisting upon the most wisely selected food exists much more than at any other time, but, unfortunately, such is not the case. The evil is general, and is as prevalent among the rich as among the poor, for there is no one class that has a monopoly of misconceptions. In the one, the fault lies in poorly selected sorts of food, in the other in deficient quantity and quality.

The ordinary home life of an infant is just as trying as his poorly adapted food. Even in his earliest days relatives and friends show a remarkable ignorance of his needs. His natural condition is one of perfect ignorance. His first acquaintance with life is a series of shocks. He is rudely exposed to heat and cold, he is too carelessly handled and tossed about, and under the plea of amusing him, various sorts of disagreeable noises are made, and equally disagreeable sights are forced on his attention. The grimaces which those in charge of him make, with the laudable intention of pleasing, are alone sufficient to frighten him. And immediately he is put under the strain of acquiring too much information. Every circumstance of his life, in the attempt to know and recognize it, requires an effort of the mind. This happens when the brain is only partly formed, is very weak, is fit only to vegetate and gather strength. During the years of its immaturity, because both physically and physiologically its constitution is not capable of much resistance, it becomes tired very easily. The ordinary efforts to become acquainted with life, to understand the seemingly involved meaning of everyday events, to accustom the senses to a useful appreciation of so-called realities, and to conform in all external ways to the requirements of civilized life, are unquestionably most trying. These efforts are continuous; there is no opportunity for intermission and rest; and therefore, the resulting strain is all the greater. For it is a well-known fact that nerve cells in young animals easily become exhausted, and most rapidly of all where the stimulus is long continued.

The most ordinary tests show this. Take a very young animal, say a dog, put him through exercises that require as much concentration of attention for a few hours as he can give, and a microscopical examination of his nerve cells will show a tired, exhausted and worn-out condition. The limits of normal fatigue are easily overstepped in any young animal, and under such circumstances, the resulting over-fatigue must be regarded as permanent deterioration. Or, subject a child to any keen impulse of excitement, such as children are allowed regularly to experience. Immediately such fatigue ensues that his ordinary capabilities act with less promptness and efficiency. He distinguishes color less easily, his skin is less sensitive, his digestion is less capable and his excretory glands are less active. This does not take into account extreme cases of shock or terror, but merely such ordinary efforts as all children are apt to undergo.

Repeated impressions on the brain tend to create a permanent condition; the wear and tear which the ordinary child undergoes is greater than people usually estimate. The mental condition resulting is, thus, far different from what the normal adult possesses. It works less clearly, less logically and at a much greater expense. All in all, it goes to form in part the child's environment, which thus becomes proportionally healthful or unhealthful. By such factors the child is affected throughout his whole life, even as far as the difference between a small and a greater power of resistance to disease, or the difference between an irritable or an equable nervous system, or even the difference between wrong and right action. Very commonly an impression upon the child is made in the way of deviations from normal standards that make life unnecessarily burdensome. And all these things, as well as countless others, can often be traced to the various forms of nutritional poverty.

To the same cause one can likewise trace much of the unhappiness of children's lives, much of their wilfulness, much of their viciousness. There are some common cases of this sort with which every one is familiar; when a baby is restless and cross, incapable of having a quiet night, the cause is usually to be found in his manner of life, as constituted by food, rest and other similar factors. An excess of starch in his food may upturn a household. Or an older child may be unhappy, poorly nourished, or even vicious. A decrease of oxygen and an increase of carbonic dioxide in the air which the child breathes makes a decided difference in the elimination of waste materials; such matter, when stored up, may produce varying degrees of intoxication, of poisoning. And as a result, his ordinary characteristics are for the time changed. With sufficient repetition, the temporary condition may become more permanent. Such changes are all the easier, on account of the profoundly mixed character of hereditary dispositions. A bias in one direction or another may be easily exaggerated into what seems a trait of profound importance. At the same time, really intelligent care could bring about quite a different result. Ordinary casual judgment would define such a child as more or less vicious, would point to any traits in the direct ancestry as the determining cause, and would congratulate itself on the advantages of scientific knowledge.

The gist of the matter is that usually too much blind reliance is placed on the commonly accepted ideas of heredity. People regularly think of the problem as a simple combination of known elements, instead of a complex process of both combination and inter-reaction of a great number of factors. Moreover, the true scope of heredity is not so great as they believe; and what is unquestionably transmissible occurs in such a form as usually to constitute a predisposition of one kind or another. The constant, countless influences of environment come in to decide upon the child's development. These influences have, as their main opponent, the theoretical intentions and academic ideas of parents and guardians; but the opposition usually amounts to little. On the other hand, the effect of environment is not to be overestimated; it acts every hour of the day, leaving impressions which, although rarely handed down to the next generation, are permanent with the individual. Parents control the bodies and minds, the hearts and souls of their children not so much by what their ancestors were as by what they themselves do and think. The results are just as sure as earlier writers, reckoning on other standards, estimated; but the method of producing the results, and the results themselves, are quite different. The direct responsibility of parents is very great, for there exists the relation of an active cause and an immediate effect. Instead of saying "Like father, like son," one rather should say, "As the father lives, so lives the son." The cases of worthy fathers having unworthy sons are usually those where the parents evoke esteem for certain laudable traits, but at the same time all the necessary conditions for the full development of the children's characters are not thoroughly conserved. A man may be a brilliant mathematician, or a profound philosopher, without necessarily showing a fitting appreciation of the physical and mental needs of his family. Proficiency in one direction does not necessarily imply an equal proficiency in others, and a bankrupt in business may be a brilliant success in rearing offspring. All in all, the general rule of the certainty of good results following careful and anxious effort holds good in the development of children just as well as in all other matters. The trustworthiness of children depends upon the elements of environment, acting upon certain inherited conditions which go to create the qualities of thinking clearly and seeing straight.

CHAPTER V

THE PLACE OF THE PRIMARY SCHOOL IN THE DEVELOPMENT OF THE CHILD

No subject concerns the interests or the sympathies of the community more closely than that of the education of children. The matter is so near to the general welfare that every possible method of interference or of development receives a warm reception. From the well-known year 1717, when Frederick William I. of Prussia promulgated his edict of compulsory education, the public attention has inclined more and more toward the view that right education of children is the basis of natural advancement. From that time, when teaching was the harbor of the unsuccessful, the incompetent and the helpless, up to the present, when its value to the community is extolled and praised, is a far cry. In correspondence to the amount of skilled thought devoted to the matter, the civilization of the world has progressed. Such men as Socrates, Aristotle, Erasmus, Bacon, Comenius, Pestalozzi and Froebel have done more than hold schools or formulate a philosophy; they have helped the civilization and culture of the world along by giant strides.

In the course of the development in teaching, the objects to be obtained have been fairly permanent; but the methods have gradually changed. All along the line the first efforts were in the way of teaching the means of communication and computation; upon these, as a foundation, were based the higher branches. In early times there seemed to be little or no problem in regard to teaching. It was required that the teacher should merely know as much of the subject in hand as he expected the scholar should learn; whether he was to teach arithmetic to children, youths, or adults seemed of little difference. On the contrary, the main idea was that a certain number of facts was to be drilled into a scholar or a number of scholars. It was thought that any one who knew these facts could, just as well as any other person, impart the knowledge, in much the same way that one woman shows another how to cook, or a blacksmith teaches an apprentice to shape a horseshoe. That there is a further element in teaching than that of simple demonstration is a very modern conception. And it is only of very recent years that even a fairly correct idea of the difficulty of educating young children has been generally felt. And even now, although some teachers and psychologists are dissatisfied with the older methods of instruction, especially in the primary schools, the large body of citizens and parents are only dimly conscious of the glaring deficiencies that are impeding the development of their children.

To a certain extent this is due to the fact that most parents at bottom regard a kindergarten or primary school as a good place in which to put their children, in order to be free for a few hours every day of the care of them. The children thereby have a means of using up surplus energy, as well as acquiring some discipline. But after all, the main object in most families is freedom from care. This has been so keenly felt that a certain successful school in New York prescribes methods of play and occupation for the greater part of the day, so that the smallest possible amount of responsibility for the proper use of the little ones' time rests upon the parents. The reason for this was stated to be the substitution of a fairly wise plan of play and work, in place of the lack of judicious supervision under which the majority of children labor. The one advantage in this state of things is that parents, when brought face to face with the problem, are apt to concede their inability or unwillingness to assume the proper direction over their children, and so, when the opportunity presents, are all the more ready to hand them over to more competent care. Naturally it is unfortunate that such a condition exists, especially as there is no inherent necessity for it, excepting the fact that parents and guardians are ignorant of where their children's interest lies, and, as a rule, have no more definite guide by which to direct their efforts than their natural affection.

Nevertheless, this spontaneous love, although generally diffused, has been at the basis of some of the greatest advances in pedagogics. This was the force which actuated Pestalozzi and his pupil Froebel. Pestalozzi in particular lacked careful preparation and careful training, and took up teaching only after having failed in attempts to make a career in other pursuits. He felt a wonderful sympathy for child-life; his love and tenderness were unbounded, and by them he held his little ones under the strongest control. "I was persuaded," he wrote, "that my affection would change the state of my children just as quickly as the spring sun would awake to new life the earth that winter had benumbed." He clearly recognized that children need something more than mere restraint and government, and what he lacked in scientific knowledge he made up in sympathetic art. "I know no other order, method, or art," he wrote, "but that which resulted naturally from my children's conviction of my love for them, nor did I care to know any other." So long as he was alone, this affection was sufficient to guide him aright in his methods of care and development, even though his equipment was meagre. But such a faculty is hard to transfer, and so his assistants — as one would expect — could not duplicate his success. When, in speaking of his school at Yverdun, he said, "the whole is pervaded by the great spirit of home union; a pure fatherly and brotherly spirit rules all," he outlined a condition that resulted from a particular agency, which could be reproduced only by a similarly gifted person. Thus it occurred under the guidance of Froebel, who, starting out as an apprentice in forestry, which he deserted for one pursuit after another, finally became a teacher at Frankfort, where his success was marked. So enthusiastic did he become, that he decided to spend two years with Pestalozzi at Yverdun. Later on he established a school at Keilhau, where he began to formulate the ideas that resulted in the kindergarten.

The advance which this institution marked was a most noteworthy one. It substituted for an unintelligent rote-method, a warm, kindly spirit of help, of allowing the budding faculties to grow with a bearable amount of freedom; it helped the child to bloom. In fact, the likeness of a child to a plant these two pioneers in education dwelt upon time and time again. They delighted in advising their audience of the necessity of carefully shielding these delicate shoots, of carefully watering and nourishing them, of sedulously freeing them from fatiguing conditions. Considered in the light of a new departure, the work was a wonderful one, marking, as it did, a revolution in accepted ideas. And if it had afterwards developed with one-half of the original force which the first leaders threw into it, there would now be no need to point with disfavor to the methods that pretend to guide our children's mental growth.

II

One of the most serious limitations of Froebel and his school was the fact that they had little of a scientific foundation upon which to base their generalizations. Their conclusions in method rested upon a foundation of keen observation, of love, of fellowship and sympathy. But they knew very little of the reasons, outside of metaphysical considerations, for their courses of work; nor were they prepared to elaborate these courses to their fullest utility and simplicity. In addition, there was a certain amount of lazy thought, of mysticism, in their belief that is almost inevitable in a new movement that evokes enthusiasm. Thus, when Froebel speaks of a young child's knowledge of number as "an essential need of his inner nature, a certain yearning of his spirit," one can see at a glance that the enthusiasm of conviction blinded his clearness of sight. Again, in speaking of his third "gift" (a two-inch wooden cube), he says that "this gift includes in itself more outward manifoldness, and, at the same time, makes the inward manifoldness yet more perceptible and manifest." This interpretation in all its symbolical amplitude might possibly suggest itself to a metaphysician who was pondering upon emblematic relations; but it would be as far from the elementary workings of a child's mind as a conception of the binomial theorem or an appreciation of the beauties of the calculus. Many of his best known disciples go to even greater lengths and construct a system of esoteric interpretations that can be equalled only by some mystic cult. Thus W. N. Hailman, in discussing the true inwardness of a wooden cylinder (second gift), says: "On revolving the cylinder on an axis parallel to the circular faces, we find that it incloses a solid, opaque sphere; teaching us the lesson, not only that each member of the second gift contains each and all of the others, but that whatever is in the universe is in every individual part of it; that even the meanest holds the elements of the noblest; that the highest life is even in what in short-sighted conceit we call death." This may be very fine as abstract thought, but considered in its relation to the rudimentary mental action of a child, it soars far above the earth.

Examples of this tendency can be multiplied indefinitely, and force one to the belief that the authors of them have set up an ideal or academic figment of child-life, a sort of glorified child-worship. In the same category must one include the deep interpretations which they give to many of the purposeless acts which are perfectly natural to infants and young children. When a baby pounds on a tin pan with a spoon or his fist, they see intelligent attempts at ascertaining characteristic qualities and reactions. When purely by chance he makes some combination of color, they point with wondering exclamations to ancestral habits showing themselves in dawning abilities. When, with the profound lack of motor coördination, which must inevitably be present in young creatures, he casually scratches some meaningless lines, they treasure up the scrawl and seek in it for indications of primeval occupations and habits. The whole mass of work is overlaid with the marks of misconception, of false ideas, of false development and growth. Even so wise a man, so conservative a thinker, so cautious a scientist as Herbert Spencer, seems to be ignorant of a baby's powers, when he advises that "we should provide for the infant a sufficiency of objects presenting different degrees and kinds of resistance, a sufficiency of objects reflecting different amounts and qualities of light, and a sufficiency of sounds contrasted in their loudness, their pitch, and their timbre." All this would be well enough, if the infant in arms had the proper physiological apparatus for carefully discriminating the various degrees of resistance, of light, of sound; or, having this apparatus, if he had the proper development of brain substance to estimate and use the results which the working of the apparatus obtained. But all this is far from fact.

The truth of the matter is that the ordinary infant is an exceedingly immature animal; that he is not only small and weak, but also he is unripe, he is undeveloped, his muscles and brain structure are imperfect, his power of coördination is very weak, and his sense perceptions are exceedingly limited. As he grows, his various faculties grow unevenly, slowly, by fits and starts. One may put various colors before him, but for a long time he is unable to discriminate between them; — one may make various sounds, but he cannot distinguish what they are, nor in many cases hear them. One may give him opportunities to develop his sense of touch, weight and temperature, but at the same time one ought to know that one's efforts are as surely wasted as attempts to cultivate a sand heap. This quality of sandy absorption — or, stated otherwise, impermeability to influences — is seen in much greater degree than most people, for the simple reason that their conceptions of infants are scarcely objective, are pre-formed, are able or willing to recognize. They have their minds made up as to what a young child ought to be, or at least what they think he ought to be. And it is with difficulty that they accustom themselves to other ideas. Even the most recent plans of primary schools and kindergarten work, although they represent great advances upon the conditions of former years, present evidences of this as clearly as one need wish to have them.

For instance, it seems perfectly natural to almost all teachers that any normal child should be able to accomplish practically any simple task or game or play-exercise. The main idea in the minds of most of them is, that the exercise should not on the surface be complex; whether the child reacts wisely and healthfully is usually decided mainly by the fact of his receiving temporary pleasure. This test is plainly fallacious, as children are constantly eager to do things which are not helpful. A child has pleasure in remaining awake at night when he should be asleep; he often delights in movements, such as rapidly whirling about as if on a pivot, which are harmful; he will repeatedly make harsh and disagreeable noises that exhaust energy much more rapidly than pleasant sounds. He may for the time being enjoy these things, or countless others like them, so that his reception of any parts of a curriculum is not necessarily a test of its real value for him. Thus he may have a certain fairly great interest in the ordinary kindergarten exercises of weaving, plaiting and threading. Nevertheless, there is little doubt in my mind that these games are decidedly harmful. In the weak and immature condition of such children's eye-muscles, body-muscles and nerve-cells, the efforts required sufficiently to perfect motor accommodation to attain the desired end must unquestionably lead to strain and consequent exhaustion. The ordinary exercises in drawing are beyond doubt useless and harmful. In its best aspect, it is merely muscle-exercise, but even as such, it is, partly from its cramped and spasmodic position and movements, decidedly deficient. In almost all cases it is the crudest sort of caricature that represents and portrays nothing. It leads to no good, and it develops no ability, but, on the contrary, elevates wrong and vicious presentments into undue prominence. When it is "directed," it is, if anything, worse; for then it receives the badge of authoritative affirmation. Unless it is the "graphic record of a perceived fact," it is worse than valueless. Naturally one cannot expect small children to perceive correctly, nor does one look to them for exact records.

In much the same way these pupils get no good from the sewing games; they should not be forced to attempt the fine movements that are required. When I have seen little ones of four and five years of age laboriously trying, by straining all their little control of body and mind, to put a too fine needle through a series of correspondingly small holes, the thought of kindness turned to cruelty, of good being twisted into bad, has always come to me. In the same category are the exercises of pricking in outline, of stringing small beads, of outlining with seeds, beads and similarly minute objects. In all these exercises a brave show is made for the edification of visitors, examiners and parents; but the benefit derived is doubtful, and although the children may seem more or less interested, — whether or not the interest is an unnaturally forced one, — nevertheless, the intended benefits are not necessarily acquired. In all this sort of work one can see that its basis is ordinary adult mental action and adult environment, but filed down and clipped off to such a body-size that its practicability, as well as its stability, has likewise departed. The method bears too much of the marks of useless pettiness, and in practice usually runs along with a commensurate absence of real spontaneity. In related ways, the uses of the sand table, while not so bad, are distinctly lacking in real freedom; there is too much confinement, too much of a pre-arranged order, too much of a lesson about it. It answers finely to take up a child's time, to "keep him out of mischief," but it is far from being a scientific foundation for broad development.

One should also find fault with the methods of story-telling now employed. With most teachers the principal test of a story is whether it holds the children's attention. This test is plainly a fallacious one, for there is, as a rule, but little reliance to be put upon a child's natural taste. There is no more reason why he should know what is best for his general intellectual welfare than that he should spontaneously recognize which is his most advantageous food. Just as when an infant, he puts everything that he can grasp into his mouth, so later he will show a keen interest in all manner of narrative, without any distinction of whether it is good or bad. Thus he will listen with absorbed attention to ghost stories, which haunt him for nights; he may like stories embodying unfavorable traits of character, as well as those which illustrate virtues. The main thing which he wants is that the story must show movement, action. He does not require sequence, order, likelihood, or a healthy development of the component events. And principally this is so, because he knows nothing of these qualities. One of his weakest spots lies in his rudimentary selective faculty. This appears to be almost equally dwarfed in his teachers, who seem disposed blindly to follow a schedule provided for them. At times the stories look as if they were expressly made for the purpose of keeping the little one from a knowledge of reality, of true relations. Instead of making the ascent from preparatory existence to real life as plain, gradual and safe as possible, they evidently seek to encumber it, to make it steep and inaccessible.

Thus, in one of the most recent synopses of kindergarten work issued this year, a list of story-games is given, showing how the narrative of the exercises should be developed. Impersonation of qualities, occupations, various characters, animals, plants, and many animate and inanimate things is the main feature. And they are all without distinction treated on the same level. Thus, a child taught in this way estimates a windmill as having the same vitality as the miller, the movements of a weather vane are just as important as the exercises held in the church below, the life of a horse as weighty as that of the husband and father who drives him. In most of these story-games there is commonly a startling look of discrimination, of healthful relations, expressed in a healthy way. Teachers regularly forget that a child is no fit person to appreciate the beautiful principle of *l'art pour l'art*. For what they are to be and think must be spread before them so plainly as to be utterly beyond the accident of misconception. These games, with all their crudeness, are far from filling the requirements. And the saddest thing of all is, that one rarely finds even in the ideas of reputedly capable teachers an inkling of the false notions which children thereby receive, nor the difficulty of unlearning a set of relations acquired when the mental life is so plastic as to be almost fluid. That even reputedly wise kindergartners are blind to this danger is seen when in a pamphlet on the subject, one of them says: "It is almost needless to add that in these games lies the life and soul of the kindergarten."

Another unestimated difficulty lies in the use of verse, mostly in the way of songs. These rhymes to an adult seem the simplest things imaginable. But they are so only when one is used to the conditions of rhymes. Any simple idea expressed in prose and in verse will make quite unlike impressions. In prose one has little in the order, arrangement or rhythm of the words to distract one's attention or to confuse the meaning. The contrary is true of verse. This is generally disregarded with children, and the natural result is that they sing and repeat words without having the faintest idea of what the meaning is; and in so singing, they are therefore going through the very process of rote-learning which the kindergarten is supposed especially to frown upon. Nothing is easier than to find many flagrant examples of this abuse; and I have seen them in every kindergarten with which I am thoroughly familiar. Even in the very simple lines in which are the verses:

> "Barrels I bind as a cooper should do;
> And hard do I labor to make them fit true,"

I found unexpected confusion. I questioned four of the children who had been singing this rhyme, and found the strangest mixture of ideas. They all pronounced the first three words as if they were only one, and they had as little conception of what one meant by binding a barrel as they had of Devonian stratification. The inverted order and the slightly unusual use of words put them entirely off the track.

This is true not only of very young children, but of children in general. They repeat words like a parrot, and very rarely stop to inquire the meaning of them. Their environment is not so arranged that they may account, as far as their primitive powers admit, for every idea, phrase and word. Often they will go for months and sometimes for years with nothing but the mistiest notions of the right significance of the verses. Not only do the exigencies of rhyme help to obscure the meaning which they otherwise might obtain, but also they tend to make the child uncertain in the daily uses of language. And not only are children of the kindergarten age so influenced, but also are those considerably older similarly affected. This was proved very clearly by the evidence of Dr. Joyce before the Manual and Technical Instruction Committee in England a short time ago. He believed that the ordinary boy is unable to understand even simple verse. As a proof, he told the Committee that he was in the habit of asking children the meaning of the following verses:

> "She is a rich and rare land,
> She is a fresh and fair land,
> She is a dear and rare land —
> This native land of mine."

Few children knew what their native land was, or what it meant, and fewer still the meaning of the adjectives. One boy thought that the phrase "fair land" meant good soil; he continued to explain that "She is a dear and rare land" meant that land was hard to get, and rents were high.

To persist in such exercises leads to the employment of words as sounds, without a concurrent growth or real understanding. The harm that this can do is not limited to the earliest years, but, on the contrary, may extend over a whole lifetime. As Pestalozzi said: "The use of mere words produces men who believe that they have reached the goal, because their whole life has been spent in talking about it, but who never have run toward it, because no motive impelled them to make the effort." This error is merely an example of the general course of training which the present kindergarten provides. All through the exercises, one can see the evidences of a conventional idea of children's development, of the ignorance of any other duty than to complete as much of a stated schedule of instruction as the time and the limited capabilities of the children admit. Whatever changes in curriculum one may think necessary are equalled or exceeded by changes in the spirit and acquirements in the instructors who have undertaken to carry it out, and any method can be administered in such different ways that often it is hard to decide where the responsibility of its good or bad results rests.

At all events, one knows that in the education — particularly the early education — of children certain facts in development and their elaborations must not be lost sight of. For example, we know that the senses develop before the higher intellectual powers, and it naturally follows that exercise of these senses goes before the more abstract lessons. Now the clear appreciation and use of mathematics — the relations of numbers — are unquestionably so abstract as plainly to be outside of the scope of the elementary school-child. It is true that children learn to count and use figures very early. It seems to be a special delight of nursery governesses and young aunts to teach little ones barely able to walk how to count up to ten, to twenty, even to a hundred, and then they point with pride to the brilliantly developing mind and the fine results of their efforts. It is true that young children can learn numbers by rote just as well as they can learn any other arrangements of sounds; but in doing so, they derive no benefit from the process, and, on the other hand, receive harm. One must keep in mind that the faculty which governs mathematical computation is located among the higher centres in the cerebrum; that this part of the brain is among the latest to attain maturity; that therefore in childhood it is in no condition to be put to a strain. Whenever a scholar at this age is forced into attempts to use this faculty, a process similar to any other sort of exhaustive work results. One can the more easily understand the inevitable outcome from a knowledge of the fact that the nerve-cells of children, being more or less in a state of unstable equilibrium, are easily exhausted, so that a consequent nerve poverty must show itself. Thus such children receive no permanent value from studies in mathematics, simple though they be; and what is more, if these studies were not begun until greater maturity, — say at least ten years of age, — not only would a vast amount of nervous wear and tear be saved, but also the children would learn as much in one year as they formerly, under the present adverse conditions and methods, learnt in five. The time thus saved might be profitably employed in strengthening both mind and body.

There are many other abuses that one can readily select from the ordinary elementary course, although because the main tendency of rational objections has now been shown, it is scarcely necessary to go over them at any length. Still, one may mention the futility of "exercises to cultivate the power of pronouncing new words with the aid of diacritical markings"[1] in the first year of the elementary course. The scholar not only must learn these arbitrary markings, by means of the worst sort of rote-memorizing, but also, if he is to use them at all well, he must show a power of observation and association far beyond his years. If the attempt is seriously persisted in, the same process of nerve exhaustion mentioned above must of necessity come about. He may gratify the pride of an examining committee and his teacher, but only at the expense of his own healthful development. For related reasons, the exercises in spelling are bad — so bad, in fact, that one should not feel the need of argument in the matter. There is before me the latest "Word Book" that is supposed to be a model for teaching the

[1] From "the latest and most advanced word-book for elementary grades."

young idea how to spell, that claims to offer "a carefully developed and progressive plan for teaching the forms and values of every-day English words." It is supposed to be used by young children, although its plan, to my mind, seems to indicate something quite different. It transgresses almost all the psychological laws of child-life that it touches, and should be regarded as an excellent means to inculcate a worthy appreciation of the difficulty of the English language. The compiler has furnished the obstacles of rote-learning, of confusing resemblances, of a meaningless accumulation of sounds, of arbitrary diacritical marks that for their learning require an adult's concentrated attention, of examples in verse and prose far beyond the scholar's years, of the multiplication of abstract rules, — of a method, in short, that is cumbersome, burdensome, unhealthy and wasteful. In a spirit of congratulation he informs us that in this wise book for children, little more than babes, "Lists of words often mispronounced are provided, together with many comparative exercises, including synonyms, words of opposite meaning, words of several meanings, words spelled alike and spelled differently. In these, as in all terms defined and in all selections for dictation, the use of diacritical marks is designed to lead naturally to the intelligent use of the dictionary."

All in all, the present methods *teach* too much, and allow too little opportunity for development.

Parents depend too much upon the teacher, and believe that their responsibility ends as soon as they hand the child over to the school. They do not with sufficient clearness see that the school rightly is no more than a means of mental discipline, and that its duty lies in building up a course in mental gymnastics. Anything else, such as looking out for the physical basis of education, is foreign to it. The prime factor of caring for every unit of energy, of avoiding every item of waste, of nourishing and protecting every budding function, in other words, of conserving nutrition, is absolutely ignored. Not only is there need of such care, but also there is a live duty to provide for it. Without such provision, the efforts of teaching not only are thrown away, but also they aid in harming the very children whom they are supposed to help. If the community has a right to insist upon the education of its children, it is natural to believe in its associated right to insist upon such prophylactic measures on the part of parents, that the children may be in proper condition to be educated. Without this, no matter what the methods of instruction are, no one can be sure that a child is being benefited. It is much on the same plan of decreeing that a man should eat a certain amount, whether or not his stomach is able to assimilate the food. If this precaution is not taken, the law inflicts useless and wanton cruelty, and instead of helping, harms.

The need for a similar care is still greater with children, for not only is their present welfare concerned, but also that of all their future connections. If a teacher saw that a pupil was so astigmatic as to render sight painful and imperfect, he would insist upon the means of investigation and relief before allowing him to continue in the class. The same reasoning applies to every part of the child's body that directly or indirectly affects the process of metabolism; and it is a prerequisite of attempts in the way of formal education to insist upon an assurance that all the child's physical functions are normal, active and healthy. If a child's nose or throat is in such a condition that full respiration is not possible, then oxidation is impaired, tissue change is unnaturally limited, and consequently mental action and development are not normal. If a child is deficient in the sugar-forming ferments, or the secretion of hydrochloric acid, or any of the constituent elements of the bile, his processes of digestion are impaired. As a result, fermentation and putrefaction of intestinal contents may supervene, with symptoms of mild poisoning. Among these symptoms one frequently sees mental torpidity or obliquity, and even viciousness. The child is backward, and so retards the whole class; he sees the teaching in a wrong light, and thus his knowledge of the matter, with the consequent development, is twisted; he feels the weight of unusual burdens, and so becomes discouraged more easily than is necessary for him.

The question of nutrition is of prime importance; in fact there is nothing in education that I know of which is more so. It includes not merely the question of food, and the right proportion of the different food elements, as well as the perfect assimilation of them, but also all the other items of distribution of body heat, of rest, avoidance of undue fatigue, recreation fit in quality and amount, the selection and variety of occupation. Not one of these considerations may with impunity be neglected, and every one of them, when rightly fulfilled, carries a proportionate amount of benefit, which will tend to make a normal, vigorous and capable adult. To put each child right in these respects provides a foundation upon which to rear the superstructure of effective educational work. But without them the teacher works against odds which are great in proportion to existing shortcomings. One must appreciate that at the start the child is heavily handicapped; that Froebel's opinion that "every child brings with him into the world the natural disposition to see correctly what is before him, or in other words, the truth," is very far from the fact. Every child has many reasons for not seeing the truth, and in most cases does not see it. If he is so nourished that every part of him works with a minimum amount of friction, the chances for the diversion of energy are lessened. It stands to plain reason that a child who suffers from an overacting heart, with the inevitable cerebral and circulatory disturbances, must be in poor condition to conduct the hard work of an organism that is growing and changing with great rapidity. In the same way, a sufferer from the air starvation which results from hypertrophied tonsils, from adenoid fungations, or one whose rest is broken, who has the obstacles of nervous irritation to overcome, cannot be fit material to go through the processes of healthful tissue change. Donaldson wisely says that "education consists in modifications of the central nervous system." Just as far as these modifications are well regulated and controlled will the child react to the normal stimuli of development.

In deciding upon the best means of developing a child, it is often wise to follow Nature's plan, — not our own. Well-founded objection has been found with the commonly received idea that a child's mind may be made to order by a schoolmaster. It seems hardly necessary to reject the imputation, although practically that is what we have been doing. On reading the dictum of so well-known a Froebelian as Conrad Diehl, one has proof of this. He says that "color is the first sensation of which an infant is capable. With the first ray of light that enters the retina of the eye, the presence of color forces itself upon the mind.

When light is present, color is present." Herr Diehl is far off the track. The retina is and must be incapable of distinguishing any color at all for some time, just as at first the ear is incapable of exact discrimination of sound, or the skin of an accurate sense of touch. To follow out Diehl's idea tends to produce the mind "made to order by the schoolmaster." Just as we know that the range of sensations of an adult is only a fractional part of what really exists, so we know that the range of a young child is proportionally limited. To found a curriculum on the supposition of full potency in the latter is stupefying to him. It directly antagonizes the growth of one of the main educational needs: the development of judgment. It is only by carefully watching the various faculties and noticing the order of their appearance, coupled with the gradual exercise of them, that the priceless faculty of exact discrimination and comparative valuation is formed. By such means it is possible to bring into life a sense of proportion, of the relative value of things. In this way a clear road may be opened up for the progress of the power to observe. And when the little one notices more and more fully what is about him, what — as he must plainly recognize — his teachers and adult connections are constantly noticing, then perforce his power of expression will likewise grow. And in the same way that it is desirable to stimulate his sense of color, so it is necessary to stimulate his other normal senses. Who shall say that a child should have a carefully developed eye, and that his ear, his taste, his senses of smell and touch, should remain crude? One may be as important as another, and all, when wisely brought out, may be made the means of a full and rounded growth. Through these faculties the child first comes into contact with the great world about him, and by the normal flourishing of *all* of them is he best able to take an adequate part in the life of the world.

Since these senses are among the first faculties to show an active growth, it follows that first instruction should be devoted to them rather than to more abstract things. In following out this idea one would, for instance, have little children use a box of colors long before they made an attempt to draw lines, or to follow drawings made in outline. Such a course would be more pleasing to them, would be more in line with their natural development, and at the same time, would remove the disadvantages arising from too early a strain which drawing puts upon the power of exact coördination. To limit them to small and exact exercises, is unquestionably harmful, for the whole mechanism of their bodies and minds calls for freedom and lack of restraint. For similar reasons the sand table should give way to a large pile of sand or dirt, where they could dig and delve, could play and build with utter freedom. If one compares the actions of a class of children working at a sand table with those seen on the sand of the seashore, or in the dirt of a garden, one will have no further need of argument. So far as possible, all unnecessary restraints should be removed. The hard confines of the ordinary room for kindergarten and elementary work should be abolished. The requirements of the word *kindergarten* should be fulfilled. Sessions should be held in a *garden*, rather than within the unlovely walls of a bleak room. The change could be easily made even in the ordinary city school. The roof, when properly enclosed, would make the finest sort of solarium, where natural conditions could be imitated with artistic and hygienic exactness. As things are now, children spend an important part of their lives in cages, the regulations controlling them are those fit for captives, and the physical discipline of making them sit in stiff and studied attitudes on poorly shaped benches is an admirable one to develop a race of puppets. There is not enough freedom, not enough spontaneity; the common function of the elementary teacher is too much that of a keeper or an upper nurse maid, and too many believe that her charges are properly influenced only when they fear and dread her.

It is not necessary to go much further into details, and one can easily follow out the main idea, and apply it to studies which come later in the school life. One must keep in mind that every subject should, in its claim for a place in the curriculum, be judged by its adaptability to the child's growth. For instance, grammar, which is highly abstract, has no place in either elementary or the so-called grammar schools. It should be confined to high schools or the secondary schools, where the mental development of the students approaches the adult form. On the other hand, the modern languages, taught not from books, but only from the conversation of walks, games, and practical "talks," might form a part of the course of very young children, whose speech centre develops very early. The resulting exercise would differ totally from the later work now done in the classic languages, which are taught as grammar is taught, and so should be kept for later years. Again, one might take up some selected work in physical geography, and so manipulate it as to make it extremely interesting and beneficial to very young children. But political geography should under no circumstances be touched until the pupil is well enough developed to understand the principles upon which the history of national life is founded.

It is an easy task to go through the regular course of studies, and select what is good and what bad, and the main factor which inevitably will lead to this choice is the better education of teachers. We must entirely get rid of the idea that any person who can pass the meagre examinations for teachers is competent to teach, and the belief that the youngest children require the teachers of least skill and ability is still more viciously harmful. Such children, who are bundles of possibilities as yet unsolidified, are the very ones who need the wisest direction. And if they were wisely directed, their later development would be much surer, better, nobler. In the face of such teaching there would be less cause for complaint, there would be less cause for men like Herbert Spencer to condemn the methods upon which the advancement of the community rests. Not unjustly does he exclaim: "What with perceptions unnaturally dulled by early thwartings, and a coerced attention to books — what with the mental confusion produced by teaching subjects before they can be understood, and in each of them giving generalizations before the facts of which these are the generalizations — what with making the pupil a mere passive recipient of others' ideas, and not leading him to be an active enquirer, and what with taxing the mind to excess, there are few minds as efficient as they might be."

CHAPTER VI

THE PLACE OF RELIGION IN THE DEVELOPMENT OF A CHILD

THERE is so much in a child's life that rests on belief, and by necessity he must be so accustomed to taking things on faith, that he of all beings seems naturally prepared to accept the religious idea and be governed by it. Moreover, he has the great forces of custom and habit, of imitation, of the weight of authority, working upon him, to the end of inducing a participation in devotional forms and a varyingly blind loyalty to certain received articles of faith. Wisely enough Maudesley has remarked: "To say that the great majority of men reason in the true sense of the word is the greatest nonsense in the world; they get their beliefs as they do their instincts and their habits, as a part of their inherited constitution, of their education, and the routine of their lives." That this is true in a large measure should not be doubted, for the evidence of it, wherever we turn, is before our eyes.

A child who is brought up in a Protestant family

looks upon the doctrine of Papal infallibility as unreasonable, while the offspring of Roman Catholic parents sees in it all necessary sanity of truth. Among the Persians, children are soothed or frightened by wondrous tales of jins and devs, which to those of occidental training seem no better than stories of fairies and gnomes. Even in the limits of a single, homogeneous people, one may find equally radical differences according to changes which lapse of time brings; among the ancient Jews before the Babylonian captivity the children grew up to believe that there were angels, but never did they have faith in the existence of devils. Even in Job, Satan was not so much of a malevolent spirit, as a fault-finding, a critical one. But after the captivity the belief in which children participated was a wider one; bad angels as well as good had their place; the idea of good and evil, of the free choice between them, of a future life in which good was rewarded and evil punished; in fact, many of the elements of a purely teleological system, the direct descendant of the religion of Zoroaster, came into Judaism. And the difference between post-Babylonian and modern Judaism is just as striking.

There seems to be in the vast majority of people a natural need for some sort of belief; an inborn desire to place dependence upon forces outside of their experience and knowledge. And this when brought into contact with environmental influences determines for ages the form of belief. Moreover, with this fact in mind it is very interesting to know that there is a remarkable similarity between most of the principal religions of the world, due partly to the fact of their common and remote descent. This is easily followed out when one notes that the direction of descent in most peoples points to that ancient mother-race, the Aryans. This people at a time when Europe was probably an unpeopled wilderness lived in Central Asia. From this starting-point emigrations took place in various directions, but mainly towards the west and northwest. Doubtless the first band was the Celts, who came to inhabit a large part of Europe. The bands that later on produced respectively the Italians, the Greeks and the Teutons followed in their various ways. One of the offshoots founded the Persian kingdom, becoming the Medes and the Persians of history; another body, having made their way north of the Caspian, developed into the Slavonic nations. Very far back Egypt received its inhabitants. And the remnant of the mother-stock overflowed in powerful bands through the passes of the Himalayas and Hindu Kush into the Punjab, and became, as Bramans and Rajputs, the dominant race in the valley of the Ganges.

These branches with a common ancestry and a common unity of past experiences bore in their customs, beliefs and language many distinguishing marks, all of which point in one direction. There is a striking similarity in their names of domestic animals and domestic life, words which they used before the time of their migrations. On the other hand, names of wild animals, of warfare, of all the countless circumstances of changed conditions, scenes and occupations vary with the time and place of their growth. In the same way they carried with them folk-tales, superstitions and beliefs that frightened, delighted and comforted them through countless ages, that served as the basis of substantial parts of their religions, that gave rise to their innumerable gods and demons, their nymphs and fauns and satyrs, their giants and trolls, their dwarfs and elves. And even to-day in our advanced civilization one can see the general beliefs covered over with marks that point unwaveringly to the dark and hidden past.

It is exceedingly interesting to compare some of the principal religions and note how many points of close agreement they have which are founded upon the most ancient myths, beliefs that unquestionably indicate a common origin and a common method of emotional excitation. For instance, the Hindoo Crishna, the Persian Mithras, the Egyptian Osiris, the Sun-gods Hercules and Dionysius, and others besides, all of whom were called saviours and worshiped as such, had much the same history. They were born on the 25th of December, the day in the winter solstice, when the sun begins its apparent annual northward journey. They all had virgin mothers, and the Scandinavian Frigga, the Buddhist Maya-Maya, the Egyptian Iris, the Hindoo Devaki, the Greek Semele, are identical. They had strikingly similar life histories, they performed much the same miracles, the number of their disciples was curiously often alike, they were persecuted, slain, and rose from the dead to ascend into heaven. A triune god was worshiped all the way from the rugged land of the Scandinavians to the fertile banks of the Egyptian Nile. And curiously enough one can trace such widely diverse systems as the ancient Greek on the one hand and more purely modern customs on the other back to a common standard in Egypt. Herodotus says that such is the source of the names of almost all the gods; the Oracles and the Eleusinian Mysteries had a like descent. And he adds that the Egyptians were the first to introduce public festivals, processions and solemn supplications, which the Greeks learned from them. Much later, after the time and writings of Tertullian, an equally strong effect was produced by this ancient people of the land of the Nile. Beliefs and conceptions of the Trinity as expounded by Egyptian theology became freely known. Isis was once more worshiped, although under a changed name, and her image, standing on a crescent moon, was almost as common then as now. "The well-known effigy of that Goddess, with the infant Horus in her arms, has descended to our days in the beautiful, artistic creations of the Madonna and Child. Such restorations of old conceptions under novel forms were everywhere received with delight. When it was announced to the Ephesians that the Council of that place, headed by Cyril, had decreed that the Virgin should be called 'the Mother of God,' with tears of joy they embraced the knees of their bishop; it was the old instinct peeping out; their ancestors would have done the same for Diana."

Instances of the prevalence of these ideas can be indefinitely multiplied. Man in a certain phase of his being is unquestionably religious. Moreover, he generally has a strain of credulity in him that readily leads him into the abuses of faith, into the ways of superstition. He has his times of weakness when he naturally turns to what seems a higher power or authority, to whom he may confess his sins whether of omission or commission, to whom he may look for praise of the good and blame of the bad, who will show a broad bosom to the sinner upon which to throw himself in times of doubt and trial. Although some of the world's great men have been religious, nevertheless, one may with safety say that the weaker the man the greater will be the likelihood of his adopting superstition instead of intelligent faith. That which has always stood before him as the head of authority and power far exceeding his own is what he is bound to pray to. Whatever credulity he may have will surely confuse senseless with reasonable authority. Whether his belief is founded upon ancestor worship, sun worship, or superstition makes very little difference. It is really not essential that there be in his creed the greatest possible approach to reason. Indeed, the very condition in which religion is commonly of most use is the one where the reason is least apt to be in full and unimpeded sway. The highly emotional states, where excitement is active, are the most favorable for the growth of religion. A man who is exalted by stimulants, by the unrestrained action of certain camp-meetings, a woman who is disappointed in love or whose emotional needs are unfulfilled, are very liable to receive an accession of faith. A man, who is crushed, who is struggling despairingly, who has been abused and harassed until his nervous irritation is pathological, is apt to turn a willing face to the promises of spiritual comfort and rest, of protection and reward for the hardships through which he has struggled. In this way belief assumes the dignity of a vital function, a phase of mind that is necessarily associated with an unstable and perturbed state of the emotions, in which whatever is affirmed positively and with conviction or whatever has had a cumulative force in the person's processes of thought comes to be accepted as proven. Thus Parker believes that "creeds — have come down to us with the force of centuries behind them. They are accepted in their traditional form chiefly because by multitudinous repetitions they have been beaten in upon the mind, and in most cases have been yielded credence without question or reasoning." Whether ethics, right conduct, be associated is really immaterial. In most religious systems it is; but the two factors may work for or against each other or quite independently of each other without either being thereby seriously affected.

These facts are of universal application, and the phases of feeling which they represent may be found among any people and at any time. They should be regarded with the utmost respect; for although they are susceptible of weak uses, nevertheless they serve at times as starting-points of some of the finest motives and emotions of which man is capable. In the same way that abnormal excitement and the consequent excesses occur in Southern and Western camp-meetings, so have like conditions taken place among savage tribes, so have happened the Siva worship in India, the fanatical allegiance to the Bacchic orgies and the pythoness at Delphi, the whirling dervishes of the Mohammedans, and the Northern Shamanism. Wherever religion is not governed by a rational idea the natural result is bound to be an excess in the way of fanaticism or superstition. The calmer and more rational side of religion represents quite a different element — that of contemplation, of philosophy, of a calm and elevated view of human relations. Such a condition is radically different from the one that produces the violent ebullitions of emotion which result in such excrescences as flagellation, as the various abuses of sexual affection. Credulity has no part in it, a blind adherence to an anthropomorphic ideal is very far from it. It represents in its best form a predominance of the nobler, the more elevated part of human nature which gradually becomes free enough to recognize the existence and the need of an ideal, and recognizing it tries to elicit a mental attitude that naturally swings in unison with it. This may most clearly be seen in prayer, which does not by any means stand for the asking of a favor or a benefit nor the expectation or wish to obtain any sort of gain; much rather does it signify the attempt to project the mind into a plane which is higher and purer than its ordinary level, to create a subjective influence that may show itself in objective action. When religion produces these results, it becomes one of the finest influences in the world, without regard to its origin or its environment.

However true this may be of adults, it does not apply to the child, and attempts to force it upon him lead to clearly unfortunate results. Only after long years of development is he able to attain the adult's religious view-point. His natural state puts him in the condition of a savage, who is incapable of attaining a fine religious feeling. The low form of emotions which he feels renders the abuses of religious feeling inevitable. His disposition is one of ignorance, of imperfectly constructed relations, of prone credulity. The crass idolatry, from which the world has in part struggled, will be the likeliest belief for his imagination to seize upon, and out of it he will construct the fabric of his religion. To him there is no inherent and reasonable distinction between falsehood and truth. He naturally inclines to superstition because its beliefs titillate his wonder-loving cast of mind. Without the restraints which mental maturity insures he is bound to fall into errors that his untried powers are sure to cause. It is just as easy for him to believe that God will kill bad little boys by a thunderbolt as it is to recognize the orderly working of an electric current. There is no doubt that he would rather believe a tale of miracles than a recital of plain facts. A tale of fairies and dwarfs is just as real to him as the recital of holy events which concern the acts of the good angels and Satan. In fact, in so far as he is normal he will want to hear stories of any sort, but mostly those which have narrative action in them. For himself he requires constant action, restraint is unnatural and becomes possible not only by practice but also by the growth of certain parts of his nervous system which are somewhat tardy in their development. For this reason, as well as on account of the natural immaturity of his mind, he is not capable of the spiritual elevation which is absolutely essential to a serviceable religious feeling. During all his childhood he remains the growing animal that knows very little of what adults call reality. He is utterly removed from the culture of to-day, he is quite unable to appreciate the advances that have been made from past standards, and the errors of undeveloped mankind are what is most natural to him. So far as his religious sense goes he is on the plane of the Terra del Fuegians who blow into the air to keep away evil spirits, or the Australian Bushmen who believe in an invisible man in heaven to whom they pray before going to war, or the South American Payaguas who bury arms and clothing with their dead to be used by them in another life. He cannot see beyond the present; the standards, the authorities, and the limitations of his existing environment seem the inevitable and the final boundaries of the universe. On the plane of them he reckons the worth and the fallibility of whatever ideas he may have. His mind is grossly receptive, not analytical, and a necessity for pure truth is not one of his needs. He is absolutely impervious to considerations of purely ideal thoughts and actions, but under stress of command and instruction may respond to them in much the same way that he would respond to any other sort of teaching. He cannot be said to have an intelligent appreciation of underlying principles; all that one may expect him to do is to exhibit a rational obedience to authoritative customs and demands. His main needs are those which provide for his nutrition; to this he is most easily amenable; beyond it his sight is dim.

It is for such reasons that his religious insight is limited and the depth of his religious receptivity is notably small. Pagan fear and pagan lack of elevation are part of the bonds that unite him to the conditions of a remote past, making his attitude that of the undeveloped heathen. His idea of God is and must be grossly anthropomorphic. He thinks of God as a big man who lives far away, and whose powers are strange and at times oppressive. He thinks of Him as a being who is moved by caprice, by anger, by cajolery, by pleasure, — in short, by the various impulses that move fallible human beings. From his guardians he readily assimilates the conception that God is constantly spying upon him in order to find out his misdeeds; his attitude towards Him is one of fear and often of repulsion. The religious adult looks to his deity for an elevating strength of soul, for the peace and consolation of spiritual communion, for an emotional uplifting that at times passes all understanding. But the child looks at Him as an adjunct to the disciplinary armamentarium of the household; he is naturally apt to regard Him as little removed from a bug-a-boo. He is totally unable, from the unripeness of his mind, to know the meaning of reverence, to feel the need of a religious growth, of even the elements of spirituality. It is perfectly true that with his faculty of crude credulity, of easily aroused fear, of inherent tendency to absorb wonder-tales and superstition, he is easily forced into a seeming respect for religious precepts and biblical personages. His faith is lightly aroused, at times, for ridiculously slight causes. But there is no solid basis to it; it is always poorly conceived, and cannot possibly appeal to his reason, or the parts of him which lead to nobility of mind and heart.

Instead of these fine influences one constantly sees grotesque effects of religious training, twisted ideas, twisted relations, twisted motives and plans of conduct that are touchingly ridiculous in the lack of consonance with the gravity of the sentiments which they caricature. It is even more touching to notice how parents, unconsciously recognizing the child's inability to absorb truly religious ideas, smile indulgently at his errors and fantastic interpretations, or with an attempt to maintain gravity of expression, seek to reprove him, and promise various and divers sort of vengeance from on high in case of infraction of ordinary rules. They rarely do anything to diminish his natural tendency to superstition, to fetich-worship, partly, it seems, because faith of any sort is apt to be thought holy, and attempts to explain matters — if only because the child cannot rightly understand religious matters — may evidently create doubt too soon in his mind.

In order to see how well this agrees with facts we need only take some characteristic anecdotes of children's religious feeling. I have tried to select such instances as appeared fair, and most of all, those said by children whose surroundings were ordinarily, or more than ordinarily, reverent. In justice I must say that in no case do I believe that the little ones bore the faintest idea of disrespect or blasphemy. They made the remarks in the best of faith, and when they fell short of piety, it was not due to intention, but rather to their evident lack of spiritual appreciation. They saw no difference between things earthly and heavenly, and honestly spoke out what was in their minds. For instance, take the case of C. J., a boy of ten years, whose general manner of life, on account of his physical delicacy, had been carefully watched. When he was told the story of Jesus walking on the water, he innocently asked whether Jesus' mother scolded him for getting his feet wet. Another child, nearly as old, was in the habit of repeating the grace before meals for the family. One day, after finishing the usual prayer, he said, with conviction that he had said those very same words time after time, that he was beginning to tire of them, that he thought God must be weary of hearing monotonous repetitions of the same idea. Principal Russell quotes a case of two boys who were talking about the rain. J. was giving whatever information he had to W., and finally said: "When the clouds are rent or opened, the rain drops out. *Rent* means *torn*, just as you would tear your clothes." W., after thinking for a time, exclaimed: "I should think God's mother would get tired mending." I remember a girl, an only child, in very good circumstances and much petted, whom I was treating for typhoid fever. Her mother had been telling her of God's great love; that even the sparrows, insignificant as they are, were included in it. The child retorted quietly: "Don't you think that God spends too much time on sparrows? If He gave a little more attention to me, possibly I shouldn't have to go for a whole month without a bit of real, solid food." Another case is that of a girl of about eleven, an unusually naïve child. Several men were sitting about the room, after dinner, discussing the Single Tax theory. One, in the course of his remarks, said: "There is not a spot on this footstool," etc., etc. The little girl, who was sitting on my knee, whispered, "What footstool?" As quietly, I explained that he referred to the earth as the footstool of God. "O-h-h," muttered the child, in astonishment. "What long legs!" Her face was perfectly grave; not for a moment did she think of irreverence. The suggested idea was that God must be an exceedingly big man.

Any one who has been much with children can multiply such instances indefinitely; they are part of their daily experience. They show how very far from the possibility of a helpful and elevating conception of truly religious life children are. It is extremely doubtful whether they are capable of anything better than a travesty on matters of really spiritual import. And whatever attempts one makes to impose upon them a system that is beyond them and to which they cannot naturally be amenable must necessarily end in distortions. Such a result is not only deplorable in itself, but also leads to misconceptions which in later life inevitably tend to lower in their estimation the value of religion and the claims which it makes. It stands to reason that when a child comes to realize the crudeness of his early beliefs, that he has been fed upon ideas which while they were represented to hold all holiness and precious truth really contain many germs and circumstances of fabled life, of error, of superstition,— it stands to reason, I say, that under such conditions his belief in the whole system must be shaken. He cannot avoid looking at it as a means of temporary control, as a thing which may be temporarily useful in controlling the passing exuberance of childish waywardness; but, at the same time, it must be hard for him to see in it the vital truth, the active principles upon which it ought to rest. And while this is unquestionably unfortunate, it would doubtless be even more so for him to continue these beliefs, which he was able to feel as a child, into the time of manhood. We unconsciously feel that the beliefs of these two times are radically different from each other, and this alone would be sufficient to prove that what we teach our children is wrong, that it must be overthrown, that we consider them incapable of participating in what seems a true and rational system of religious faith. If they are to have any such code at all, it must be one which is just as true for their early as their later years. And so long as this is impossible, so long as the unripeness of their minds and their generally undeveloped state forbid the grasping of a full-grown system, then something else which has more of stability and as much of disciplinary features should take the unfilled place.

As one would logically expect, children are especially liable to the various excesses which result from the perturbed condition of their unstable emotional and imaginative natures. One does not look to them for keen discrimination between what is reasonable and what is unreasonable, nor for an exact separation of illusive subjective conditions from more rational objective circumstances. Concrete cases of the abuses of religious feeling one finds easily enough. They occur in every community and every age, wherever a child is found whose sensitive nature receives so strong an impulse as to be forced out of the line of ordinary conduct.

Such instances as that of "The Welsh Fasting Girl," of children who believe that they are called upon to show some miraculous power of divine intervention, as that of Bernadette Soubirous, who not many years ago founded the wonder-working shrine at Lourdes. The case of this child while not more remarkable in its genesis than that of many others, is interesting on account of the widespread results of her peculiar mental condition. She was a plain, simple village maid, of a strongly mystical cast of mind, whose circumstances were the usual ones of her class. She had heard much about saints and miracles and was deeply impressed by the stories about them.

One day she went about her usual duty of gathering wood. On the way she had to cross a stream, and began to take off her stockings. As she stooped down she became conscious of a presence that suddenly made itself manifest before her, and when she regarded it fully she saw a wonderfully beautiful woman whom she knew immediately to be the Virgin. The brilliant loveliness of the figure was beyond her powers of description or even full recognition. It was, as she thought, superhuman, God-like. The girl fell upon her knees and worshiped in adoration. At later times she again saw and even spoke to the apparition. Her relatives and friends at first ridiculed her accounts, and even tried to persuade her that she was deceiving herself as well as trying to deceive them, that she saw visions and dreamed dreams. But Bernadette knew better; she was as certain of the Virgin's visit as she was of her own existence, as she was of the divine command laid upon her to build a church. And finally her faith was rewarded by full belief. For the vision came to her at last in the presence of her mother and some neighbors. The child fell upon her knees, with clasped hands and raised eyes, her face lit up with the light of ecstacy. Although the attending witnesses saw nothing but a kneeling girl with a glorified face, they felt sure that the change in her must have been the work of a divine power. After that everything was plain; belief bred belief; credulity like a contagion infected almost every one it touched, and the world has become familiar with Bernadette's holy spring and its associated miracles.

The spectacle of praying, fasting, ecstatic, exalted children is not rare; nor is it rare to see them afflicted with various emotional derangements which one can trace to disturbances more or less directly attributable to premature religious excitement. Such efforts are, of course, to be deplored. But it is just as sad to see these irresponsible persons forced into the most solemn covenants, the sacredness of which they are totally unable to comprehend. Even at twelve, thirteen and fourteen years, the age at which children are commonly confirmed, the imposition of obligations and the accompanying eliciting of promises that are supposed to rest upon a foundation of intelligent understanding are not, to say the least, a serious preparation for a useful and beautiful life. For no ordinary boy or girl can at such a time know the meaning of the ceremonies at which he assists, he cannot understand the foundation upon which they stand nor the length and breadth of them. He subscribes to the required formulas in much the same way that he would take part in the commencement exercises of his school, or in any function which has the surroundings of pomp and circumstance, backed up by the commendation of friends and relatives. When in later years he attains the age of fuller understanding and discretion, he cannot possibly feel more reverently and think more highly of a system which extorted promises from him at a time when, swayed by considerations of emulation, example and obedience, he vowed to be and do things the meaning of which he knew not. Such a course, instead of making loyal and zealous communicants and adherents, is more apt to render them lukewarm and antagonistic. In place of open-hearted and reverential believers who feel in every fibre of their being the conviction and truth of their faith, in place of inspired adherents whose lives represent the essential excellence of a prayer, one commonly sees bodies of men and women in whose allegiance to creed social considerations, worldly considerations, and reasons of inertia have an unfortunately large share.

There is a place for a related training of children:

that of morals. That is the proper sphere in which they can normally and healthfully be led as well to their own advantage as that of the community. For them especially is the remark true, that conduct is three-fourths of life. They come upon the world's scene in a condition of almost neutral plasticity. They may have various inherited leanings and predispositions which, if allowed unimpeded growth, would doubtless turn them in definite directions. But the organization of family and social life does not permit unimpeded growth of any characteristics. The whole tendency is a modifying one, a tendency towards a certain common similarity. This tendency varies with the peculiar constitution of the child's immediate environment, so that we finally have the problem of a mass of more or less dimly inherited leanings combined with a particular set of surroundings — the whole of which goes to make up the person as he grows into adult life. One of the things which bring out the weak spots in the combination is the fact of a certain indefiniteness in our moral life, a lack of directness and steadfastness which children appreciate very keenly. For they learn conduct in the same way as they come to know relations in space or the qualities of physical bodies, that is, by the experience of unconscious absorption. Thus they realize gradually, and I may say insidiously, that there is a disparity between teaching in morals and conduct in their daily life, that ideals, which are not by any means acted out by those who pretend to advocate them, are placed before them as final. To say that we should give our coat to him who takes our cloak is all very well if we follow the idea to its logical termination. But it falls far short of having good effect when we seek by every possible means to hunt down and punish the taker. To say that we should try by all odds to do unto others as we would have them do unto us is very fine, so long as we do not, by contrary conduct, give the lie to the teaching. To say that the poor, on account of their poverty, have a better chance of salvation than the rich smacks strongly of virtue. But the anticlimax comes with crushing force when children every day of their lives see the people who preach the doctrine bending the ready hinges of their knees before men of wealth that power may come with crawling. In short, a large part of ethical teaching is purely didactic, does not embody actual practice in life, and therefore children receive it more as they receive abstract propositions than as living facts.

An easily apprehended reason why children's moral training should consist largely of applied ethics is the fact that they understand and assimilate concrete results much sooner than the theoretical rules which underlie them. The growth of the brain is such that the parts of the cerebrum which have to do with the elaboration of abstract matter is very slow, is about the last to reach fruition. One may not expect children to have reasonable conviction, but one may be sure that they will readily enough follow repeated examples. Therefore one must necessarily believe that all such abstract matter is not only absorbed with the greatest difficulty, but also is most easily distorted. There must be a constant atmosphere of the moral life which the child is supposed to have. From this atmosphere will come much better results than from any amount of teaching to which he may be subjected. The matter comes down to a question of direct responsibility of the child's parents and connections, for they are the patterns which are most closely followed, simply and plainly because they are the models which childish imitativeness must surely follow. It is only necessary to remember that the order of development in very young children is first of all the automatic ganglion centres of the viscera, of the heart and of the lungs; then the spinal cord controlling the movement of the limbs; then the centres of sensation; and last of all, the centres of ideation, of thought, of will. These last-named centres do not reach their full development until from twenty-five to thirty-five years of age. Their action before that time is not fully reliable. And processes which are dependent upon them must be consequently incomplete. But the domain of conduct, especially in young persons, is generally not so much the realm of thought as of imitation and example, while that of religious conviction is, or should be, one of

THE PLACE OF RELIGION

thought, judgment, not a blind following of what somebody else has said or felt.

As children learn conduct by direct imitation, they should have their models constantly before them, and these must be supplied by the persons who help to form their environment. It will not do to act in one way and instruct them to act in another; to have one standard for oneself and quite another for them. This is what parents and guardians with more or less pretence regularly do. Children, with their acute, unconscious susceptibility to influence, notice the discrepancy with the greatest ease. And naturally they do not take the prescribed rules in too serious a light. They openly regard them either as purely theoretical and of little importance, or else as ideas which outwardly they must respect, but inwardly may with safety ignore. The standard of domestic virtues, of self-restraint, of amiability, is none too high; by such means it is kept conveniently low. At the same time, the formation of the general character advances with an equal pace and is similarly retarded. Worldly wisdom, so-called, which too often is merely a synonym for insincerity, deceit, or even dishonesty, is early noticed and too easily assumed. In a few years so much harm is done that only the most strenuous exertions can undo it. But these are not supplied; on the contrary, the old ideas are with greater force than ever insisted upon as essential to social and business success.

At an early age the matter is in all likelihood made worse by the teaching of some one of the various creeds. What the child is most impressed by is the part of it which includes an element of mythology, or an element of terror, or an element of narrative interest. His fears as well as his faculty of enjoyment are played upon; his teachers seek to lead him through the deep mists of superstition into the clear air of a reasonable and ennobling belief. How far they succeed Galton testifies to when he laments that what the world needs is not so much a greater intellectual progress as a better growth of character. Strangely enough, educators feel most anxious to help along the former rather than the latter; and in this anxiety they have, by experience, discovered certain rules and laws of the child mind. One of them is that practical examples and concrete instances in a scheme of instruction come before the theoretical and abstract generalizations called rules upon which they are based. There is hardly a teacher of arithmetic in the land so uninformed as not to have heard of this idea, even if he may not use it, and there are almost as few who disagree with it. Nevertheless, a parity of reasoning in religious instruction is clear. And, in this connection, there is an even greater necessity for the application.

Applied ethics represents the concrete example; creed religion may be taken as the philosophical generalization. Such is the order in which they fall;

and so placed, the value of both of them is undoubtedly great. When a person has arrived at the age of independent thought, when he is past the time of the arbitrary support which a system of real morals gives, then he is fit for the more philosophical, more intellectual part which purely religious belief in its best sense ought to bring. In the meanwhile, parents and guardians must know that they are directly responsible for the ethical conduct and the moral status of their little ones. Their every act has its bearing, just as every touch of a potter's hand has some little share in the final result of his work. The constant repetition of such acts goes to make up a child's personality. Doubtless such repeated acts count for more in the long run than isolated examples of a virtue that may be great but is not a matter of every-day occurrence. The earth is devastated by a flood, it is strengthened and made fruitful by countless minute raindrops.

CHAPTER VII

THE VALUE OF THE CHILD AS A WITNESS IN SUITS AT LAW

IT is a rather strange fact that courts of justice, whose administration is one of the most important functions of society, should have shown such a variety of opinion in regard to the right value of children's evidence. There are so many cases where such evidence is of the most vital importance that the need of settling the question once for all is undoubtedly great. Nevertheless, authorities on Evidence, possibly feeling how shifty the matter is, have given it a wide berth. The subject has very many times come up for discussion, but has never been settled. The drift of opinion of to-day is somewhat farther advanced than in former times; but the advance has been wavering, tentative, not based on a solid foundation of knowledge. As far back as 1779, the judges in R. *vs.* Brazier, 1 Leach, Cr. Cas. 199, held that "an infant, though under the age of seven years, may be sworn in a criminal prosecution, provided such infant appears, on strict examination by the

Court, to possess a sufficient knowledge of the nature and consequences of an oath, for there is no precise or fixed rule as to the time within which infants are excluded from giving evidence; but their admissibility depends upon the sense and reason they entertain of the danger and impiety of falsehood, which is to be collected from their answers to questions propounded to them by the Court." Here the crucial idea is that the evidence is more or less reliable, not so much on account of the child's capability to see, think, and narrate clearly and honestly, but merely on the ground of having enough religious or moral training to appreciate the "danger and impiety of falsehood."

The point is still more strongly stated in Best's work on Evidence (I. 241). This authority lays down the rule that "when a material witness in a criminal case is an infant of tender years, the practice has been for the Judge to examine him, with the view of ascertaining whether he is aware of the nature and obligation of an oath, and the consequences of perjury. And if it is ascertained before the trial that a material witness is of tender years, and devoid of religious knowledge, the Court will, in its discretion, postpone the trial, and direct that he shall in the meantime receive due instruction on the subject." That this rule was not always followed is clear enough, for the author shortly afterwards cites a case, where Alberson, B., refused to postpone a trial for the purpose of giving religious instruction to a witness of twelve years of age, since "all the Judges were of opinion that it was an incorrect proceeding; that it was like preparing or getting up a witness for a particular purpose, and on that ground was very objectionable." Another authority, Greenleaf, makes a similar rule (Evidence, I. 367): "If the child, being a principal witness, appears not yet sufficiently instructed in the nature of an oath, the Court will, in its discretion, put off the trial, that this may be done." This seems fairly definite, except the phrase "sufficiently instructed in the nature of an oath." Here the element of religious training comes up once more, and is so really misty that it is bound to cause disagreement. Greenleaf proves this almost immediately after stating his rule, by citing the case of R. *vs.* Williams (7 C. and P. 320). Here he states that Patterson, J., in rejecting as a witness a child of eight years of age, said that he "must be satisfied that the child felt the binding obligation of an oath from the general course of her religious education, and that the effect of the oath upon the conscience should arise from religious feelings of a permanent nature, and not merely from instructions, confined to the nature of an oath, recently communicated for the purpose of the particular trial." As if to show how easily such rules as above quoted may be overturned, the Code of Criminal Procedure of the State of New York, 1897, makes some radical changes; it speakes of a greater age as necessary, and attempts to eliminate the religious factors. "Whenever in any criminal proceedings a child actually or apparently under the age of twelve years, offered as a witness, does not, in the opinion of the Court or Magistrate, understand the nature of an oath, the evidence of such a child may be received though not given under oath, if, in the opinion of the Court or Magistrate such child is possessed of sufficient intelligence to justify the reception of the evidence."

All through the course of these changes one can see the predominance of the religious idea, and until very late days, the usual grounds for rejecting the evidence of children were (1) want of religious knowledge, (2) want of religious belief, (3) refusal to comply with religious forms. Evidently jurists recognized the unreliable nature of the communications, and while not knowing exactly where to lay the blame, nevertheless tried to erect some sort of barrier to limit the evil. This is one reason why so many contradictions in rulings, of which there is a wealth, exist. For instance, in the case of R. vs. Holmes, quoted in Taylor's Evidence, the presiding magistrate considered a certain child competent to testify, because she told the Judge that she said her prayers, and thought it wrong to lie. On the other hand, Wharton quotes a case of a girl three years older, whose testimony was rejected because she knew nothing of future rewards and punishments.

The strangest part of the subject — for as a rule the law does not lack for safeguards against most of its enactments — is that no serious attempts have been made to find out why and how far this sort of evidence is not trustworthy; and if this had been done, there would be no need for citing such well-known cases as that of Dr. Laurent, where a boy of thirteen years accused his father and twelve other men of a murder which they clearly did not commit; nor such a case as was recently reported in the daily press, where, in a suit for divorce, two little sisters gave diametrically opposite accounts of the domestic relations of their parents, although the only active cause for an utter disagreement in testimony was a difference in sympathies. The father's partisan saw the mother's acts in an unfavorable light, while the account of the other child entirely reversed the relations of praise and blame. Still, there is no reason to doubt the little ones' honest wish to tell the truth. The trouble lay not in their intentions, but rather in their particular manner of judging. This last-mentioned case, instead of being remarkable, is really what one ought to expect, because a truthful and faithful narration of events or a condition is no easy matter, even for many adults; for a child it is exceedingly difficult, and in many cases impossible.

There are many reasons, looking to the mental and physical condition of the child, why this is so. As was seen in the first chapter, the development of the brain is very slow, and even after its gross form develops, a long time must elapse before the finer structure becomes complete. It is by this finer structure that its highest work is done. This applies especially to the intermediate regions in the cortex, called the association centres, where the various functional areas meet, and where the characteristic memories are stored up. So long as these centres are unripe, and they certainly are in such condition until puberty at least, the ordinary impressions do not become sufficiently marked, nor can they be fully recognized and expressed by the child. It is much on the plan of a series or network of communicating canals. If the trenches are completed only in separate spots, no steady stream of water can flow through them, and no matter how well the work in these various areas has been done, the full results of the undertaking do not come into existence until every connection is finished.

One constantly sees proof of this in the child's clumsiness, which is apparent in mind as well as in body. It is only after months of trying that he is able to use knife and fork gracefully and efficiently; it is only after years of effort that he is able to write readily, to perform many of the most ordinary acts of life. One expects this, and so one does not notice it. One does not stop to think that what he does well is what does not require a careful self-consciousness or concentration. Moreover, he is helped by his ignorance; he cannot fear that of which he knows naught. Fear does not make him cautious, and therefore correspondingly incompetent. His successful efforts are first confined to the purely somatic functions and physical acts; after them, by a long distance, comes intelligent mental effort.

Now a word is a more or less complex idea composed of more than one sort of image. The simplest word has a host of associations which require for their proper tabulation considerable time and experience. As an example, take the word *milk*. This will bring to mind the ideas of fluidity, of food, of the bottle from which the child has taken it, of color, of cows, of farm life, of wagons, and horses, and so on to an indefinite extent. Other words are similarly multiple in their concepts and suggest many diverse images. In an immature condition, where the effects of experience and practice are small, it is difficult to keep these various concepts in their proper relations. Like a wagon wheel slipping into a rut the mental impulse deviates from its path. Consequently any certain impressions may be distorted to widely removed conclusions. So long as there is not a direct connection between a concept and its rightful expression, no serious reliance should be placed upon the person's testimony. This is exactly the condition of children. The difficulty of learning each separate word is really great, but after this is done, the task of learning simple combinations still remains, and as the child grows older, the necessity for increasing his vocabulary advances at a greater rate. The acquisition of this knowledge comes in a slow and fragmentary manner. For a long time it resembles a sort of patchwork, and not until after the lapse of years does it become homogeneous. During all this time not only are the child's concepts imperfectly formed, but also his expressions of them must be still more imperfect. This is so true that unconsciously one acts upon it, and is much astonished if a child expresses himself well and clearly, while on the other hand, one is amused and tolerant of grotesque expressions. In fact, most of the quaint and witty sayings of childhood are never intended as such, and the laugh which they provoke is as astonishing to the little one as the remark in question is to the auditor. They should be regarded merely as tentative efforts after ordinary expression, and the humorous part results from the child's misapprehension of normal relations.

Proofs of the truth of this we meet every day, and an occurrence in my own experience is a case in point. I was walking one day with a little girl, past an oyster restaurant, on the window of which was displayed the sign, "Families supplied." The meaning to an adult is, of course, perfectly plain; but with the child it was quite different. Immediately after reading it, she clapped her hands, and cried out: "O! let's go in and get a little baby. I've wanted a baby brother for a long time." Again, another case is one quoted by Principal Russell. It was a case of a boy of ten years who thought that when a person boarded with another, he went to the latter's house, and pounded with his fists on the wall of a room. Another child of nearly eight years of age, wrote his name with the title "master" before it. On being asked the meaning of the prefix, he said, "That's because I'm master of something, — my dog." It must be remembered that these are not extreme cases, but rather such as happen every day. They show how very crudely children express themselves; how far away from having and expressing an exact idea they are. Now, if so much difficulty opposes them in single words, how much more burdensome must be the obstacles in trying to give a sustained and truthful narrative! The task is greater than one ought to expect of these little people.

If this were the only trouble, it would be great enough, but it is only one of many. The most ordinary things, as well as the most unusual, lead to misconceptions that may give rise to totally false interpretations. The child is thus in danger of extracting a meaning from conversations or events that is not at all justified by the circumstances. His report of such things is correspondingly distorted. I remember showing a boy how to look through a microscope, and drew his attention to a budding yeast plant that was fixed on the slide. Some fancied resemblance caught his eye, and later on I was astounded at hearing him tell his father that he had seen a little bit of a goat through the instrument. The child was far from wishing to deceive; he was simply misled by an imperfect understanding of things, which could never have occurred to an adult, even to one who knew nothing about the yeast plant.

One of the hardest things for children is to concentrate their thoughts and attention. They are easily distracted from any matter in hand, and besides, commonly observe things very inaccurately. Like the flitting of wind-blown leaves, their thoughts and glances swing this way and that, resting for a short time, and very lightly, on many unconnected places. The inferences which they naturally draw must therefore be false. Things widely diverse in their constitution, but having some trivial thing in common, will appear to their unobserving eyes as similar; and, for instance, they would claim decidedly to identify a man simply because some easily marked characteristic, such as baldness, struck them as familiar. Here one can plainly see the characteristic workings of poorly connected association centres. For related reasons they observe things poorly, and though they look with seemingly sufficient intentness, nevertheless, they do not see enough. Their reasoning consequently is faulty, and they ascribe causes to phenomena that strike us in commonplace circumstances as ludicrous. Thus a boy of ten and one-half years, gravely explaining why dogs kept their mouths open, said that it was due to hunger, and that in this way the animal was most ready to snatch up a bit of food; and another child of ten years announced that all small teachers were cross, while tall teachers were good-natured. He had drawn this general conclusion and opinion from his experience with two young women, who formerly had taught him. In the particular connection quoted, these methods of forming conclusions are of little importance; but when they are translated into serious evidence, which is bound to affect other people's interests, they open the way to great misconception and injustice.

Going back once more to the unripe condition which is characteristic of the youthful brain, one finds such things perfectly natural. The various constituent elements of the adult nervous system are present, but in such an undeveloped state that to expect complete responses to demands made upon it, would be just as unreasonable as endeavoring to pay off a large indebtedness with a small capital. When ganglion cells are only partially formed, when their prolongations exist merely in a rudimentary form, when their histological elements are in part lacking, it is absolutely necessary to conclude that functional activity is likewise affected.

Thus the idea that children naturally tell the truth is in itself far from true. To say that "children and fools don't lie" merely means that they have not so many of the ulterior reasons for deceit that actuate adults. As a matter of fact, it is natural for them spontaneously to tell untruths. In addition to their physical limitations, they have deficiencies in experience that are dangerous to seeing and telling things correctly. The difficulties of ordinary sight are overcome very gradually and after years of trial. One can appreciate this easily enough when one thinks of the obstacles in the way of ordinary or upright vision. The human eye is constructed on the principle of a compound lens, and the resulting vision is projected upon the retina inverted. A person looking at a chair really sees it upside-down, and the time which is necessary to learn the association of an upright position and an inverted image is undoubtedly great. The process is so elaborate that one, thinking about the matter, is surprised at the uniformly fair results that adults attain. The experience comes slowly, and as the result of countless movements of touching, lifting and moving. The partly developed brain does not act logically, and has to learn as if by rote the most ordinary facts in nature. Little by little such facts are assimilated, little by little the child emerges from the mists which envelop his early faculties. Only in the most gradual way does he come to associate the visual impression with the proper relations of the object in space. This difficulty, added to his limited power of accurate observation, is bound to make his reports unreliable. This disability is increased by the trouble which he inevitably encounters in understanding the third dimension. For a long time, he practically does not know of its existence, and even when he learns something about it, he uses the knowledge very crudely. The existing lack of perspective shows itself in his attempts at drawing, for, outside of any technical knowledge, he is unable, even at a rather mature age, to see the difference between flat lines and those drawn in projection.

Growing knowledge of size and position brings its penalties; he measures things by his own small standard, not by the adult. Things seem great, even formidable to him; his imagination is deeply impressed. The idea of formidable size easily changes into that of the grotesque,—especially in a mind that is ignorant of the true connection between cause and effect. That is one of the reasons why our little ones so readily incline to a belief in ogres, giants and monstrous forms. In addition, this quality falls very congenially into place beside that of irresponsibility. The child delights in what to us is unreal, in "make believe." The flights of fancy conjure up other and strange worlds, which are as real to him as the world about him, where things are topsy-turvy. Here events come in strange and wonderful ways; the little one becomes a hero or a victim; he encounters experiences the half of which is beyond all fact. For him there is no hard and fast limit; there is no end to what is possible. The fears of a mythical dragon oppress him just as much as a real danger; and ordinary things inspire the same emotions as the grossest figments of the imagination. A dream, a story, or a vision started by some fugitive train of thought is as apt to induce a steadfast belief, to which he will hold with the fullest force of conviction, as a real series of actual happenings will cause in an adult. I know of tales of severe punishment or ill-treatment, reported in this way by school-children at the hands of teachers, which investigation proved to be utterly without foundation. And I remember accounts of pursuits by wolves, bears and griffins, which were reputed to have occurred in the streets of New York, told to me with all the force of righteous conviction. Questioning, without an emphatic statement of disbelief, is apt to confirm these opinions, with the result that a child who is supposed to be all purity, guilelessness and truth, may accomplish the ends of a hardened perjurer. But so easily is his mind influenced, that expressed doubt or disapprobation will make him utterly repudiate the whole story.

A characteristic quality of childhood that is capable of causing much mischief is its vanity. The child regularly imagines himself as the doer of great and impossible deeds, as the holder — according to his lights — of important functions. He knows nothing of the necessity of effort, of striving; he associates the desire for a thing with the immediate fruition of that desire. His treatment at home during his very young childhood helps to strengthen the tendency. His experiences, all the way from being constantly called a "big man," to hearing outlandish tales, are regularly of this sort. Very rarely does one see an effort made to develop a sense of proportion. Parents and attendants feel satisfied if by cajolery and by flattery the child makes only a bearable amount of trouble. They know that by such means they can hold his attention and keep him quiet, although they are thereby far from improving his moral condition. A certain amount of vanity is natural to every one; and at times we find this ordinary amount largely increased in occasional persons, who should be regarded as illustrations of the persistence of youthful types. Thus one hears of women who bind and maltreat themselves, of girls who write love-letters to themselves, and thereon base a story of a fortunate engagement to marry; in the same way, and with as little basis in fact, children will at times recount with every show of truth tales of happiness or unhappiness, of kindness or abuse. Here again they may have no intention to make others bear the responsibility of fancied deeds; they merely feel the need of satisfying their vanity, of calling attention to themselves, of being pitied and petted. When brought into a Court of Law, such traits are capable of working untold harm — even of wrecking innocent lives.

Everybody is familiar with the imitative faculty in children; every one knows that they follow closely after examples which they see before them. Practically, we know that this is a fact, and theoretically, it is as it should be. All young creatures must be imitative in order to live, and no one would expect that this faculty would stop short at any exact and designated limits of safety. As a matter of fact, there is an active tendency to ape the ways and manners of those about them, as well as to be more or less impressed by a startling occurrence. In this way I have seen a girl of twelve years counterfeit exactly all the symptoms which her sister showed in an attack of hip-disease; moreover, I was not certain of the counterfeit nature of her condition until the administration of an anæsthetic, after which no deception was possible. In the small things of life the force of this faculty is constantly felt, so much so that it affects the most fundamental habits. The ideas of the growing child are surely thus regulated, so much indeed, that one can hardly speak of his having an independent mental life at all. He takes his tone from his environment just as surely as he acquires his speech and manner of expression.

To a large extent his mind is a blank, an untilled field, and the impressions made upon it are the means of cultivation. In so far as he is developed at all is he thus influenced. Therefore he is being moulded every day and every hour; but most of all is he affected when some important event happens which makes him incline in whatever way the sympathies and interests of those about him dictate. As a result, quite outside of the question of honest intentions, his view-point is not shaped so much by the actual course of events as by the interpretation which those nearest to him put upon them.

That element in making evidence trustworthy, the realization of the nature and obligation of an oath, is one of the most difficult to make sure of in a child's testimony. Lawyers have insisted upon exacting this without knowing positively whether the child were capable of it. Whenever in the conduct of a cause a doubt arose, it was in relation to the one particular case at issue rather than to the whole body of cases. In the same way, some question may have arisen concerning the religious training of the one child on the stand rather than of all children in general; and an unfortunate feature of the matter is, that attorneys, in trying to have a child's evidence admitted or rejected, are apt to base their arguments, not on some principle of impartial truth, but merely on considerations of the client's interest. But without doubt some idea of the fallibility of this element has been prevalent in the general legal mind, for almost all cases in point have brought out objections from one side or the other against the testimony of such witnesses. What is needed is a full and definite knowledge of the reasons why a child is unable reliably to fulfil all the important duties of a witness. To realize the nature and obligation of an oath requires more than an understanding of certain religious forms, or even of religious ideas. Such ideas, as was shown in the last chapter (Chapter VI.), exist as a mood, as a more or less artificial condition. The binding formula of swearing a very youthful witness cannot be any greater than — even if it is as great as — an ordinary injunction against lying. For one cannot expect him to be held by reasons which are beyond him. His idea of the Deity is decidedly anthropomorphic; to him God is a big man, with all the weaknesses and passions of mortals. The pure, abstract idea of divinity is far and away from him. He feels the assurance of divine care for the world and interest in him only on the plan that he regards the affection of his father, but with one great distinction; requiring a tangible method of appeal to his senses, he understands and appreciates in a partial sense his parent's interest and authority, whereas he sees, feels, and knows nothing about a God, excepting what people have told him. The all-important elements of appeal to his comfort, his physical well-being, are immeasurably stronger in the case of his parent than his God. His greatest respect for the latter is apt to be founded upon a blind fear, the dread of a promised punishment. Naturally, it is unnecessary to say, obedience founded upon such motives is very easily distorted, so that he most easily responds in the way that he believes will be most pleasing.

The sanctity of an oath represents one of the highest developments of civilized life. It involves the sacrifice of personal bias, of personal welfare, of personal relations — the very things which go to make up the child's little life. It calls for a foundation of principle, of which children are naturally ignorant, and an elimination of expediency, which is commonly the governing factor with them. Likewise it presupposes a sufficiently wide experience, a sufficiently broad training in conduct, so that a partial knowledge at least of what justice means may result. A person who, from his position, cannot have a proper respect for consequences, is, when so placed that he may by his irresponsible words sway the outcome of important causes, a positive menace to particular and general interests. This is the position of the child-witness; for his experience has been so circumscribed, so closely restricted to his own physical needs, pleasures and gratifications, and the bent of his mind calls so clearly for tangible evidences and reasons for things, that he is the last one to feel the influence of purely abstract considerations.

Another fact which one must keep in mind is, that the child knows nothing and cares nothing about the public tone. The ordinary man knows and appreciates the value of public morality and right dealing, he has a pride in the high standard of the community's acts. He is aware of the part he must play in order to maintain this standard, and that the resulting praise or blame affects him as well as his fellow-citizens. He knows that there is no such thing as private virtue and public vice, and therefore, he has a distinct reason to hold on to what is good for the state, and to discard what is bad. But a child is absolutely ignorant of all this. So far as he is concerned, the community does not exist, its welfare is nothing, its aims and ends for him are nothing. He looks merely for the approbation of parents and guardians, for they constitute his little world. Any authority outside of them is merely a force with which to frighten or coerce him. The sentiment of patriotism, when it exists in him at all, is merely a reflection from the light which shines from some of his connections. In himself he is plain darkness, to whom the light comes in feeble and uncertain rays. His position of neutral dependence requires an unquestioning willingness to follow in an indicated path, no matter where it may lead. If it tend in the direction of the public elevation, well and good; but if it stretch out in the opposite direction, he treads it as willingly. He rightfully has no part in any public function, except a decorative part, and the narrow scope of his whole life makes certain a like narrowness of ideals.

Outside of these somewhat theoretical reasons, there are certain physical conditions found in childhood, which so easily become pathological that abnormal mental action results. In the first place, the intestinal tract does its work of digestion and assimilation when its contents are relatively quite or nearly aseptic; as soon as there is a slight excess of fermentation or putrefaction, pathological manifestations result. These conditions one should regard as mild but true cases of real poisoning, with characteristic mental as well as physical symptoms. If a child were made sick by some familiar poison, no one would for a moment think of placing reliance upon the disordered thoughts and expressions that resulted from the pathological effects of the intoxication. Children are peculiarly susceptible to these effects, and respond to them very strongly, partly because of their slight power of resistance, and partly because the false mental actions which they induce seem just as reasonable to their inexperienced judgments as the ordinary facts of life. The slighter cases of poisoning caused by intestinal disorders act in the same way, and with as much certainty. Thus a child suffering from these disorders, absorbing poisonous products of fermentation, will see or hear or feel or dream of things and actions which he may honestly translate into terms of actual experience. He may be as sure of this as of any reality, and still the whole matter may have no greater foundation than the undigested starch in a banana which he ate between meals. The various chemical processes of assimilation, which easily fall into disorder, may act as irritants either in the way of repressing normal impulses, or exaggerating sensory impressions. There is really no limit where this process may end, nor do we know the fixed point where it must begin. At all events, we do know that the chemical reactions in assimilation are exceedingly complex; that they are easily interfered with; that the resulting products and by-products are very diverse, and in some instances poisonous. In this way the relation of concepts may be broken, and the consequent mental impressions may even go so far as to assume the dignity of full illusions.

Sometimes the ordinary methods of teaching, of learning by rote, are at fault. These act in the way of subjecting the nervous system to a strain which it is poorly prepared to stand. Its normal sphere of activity lies in acquiring new impressions that should vary so regularly as to avoid the danger of monotony. Impressions that are repeated too often bring about a morbid, nervous condition that has been called "psychical trauma." If such a condition exists, it may debase intellectual powers to much below their rightful standard. Outside of distinct mental disorders, classified as diseases, some of the lower emotional and mental activities may in a similar way be markedly injured. One has evidence of this from such signs as nervous digestive disorders, hysterical attacks, loss of sleep, otherwise inexplicable, disturbances of flushing and pallor, loss or impairment of reflexes. One sees these manifestations every day, and the task of connecting them with impaired intellectual activity is not hard. The tender nerve cells have no large amount of reserve energy, and what they possess is easily exhausted. Monotonous strain, instead of giving them the strength which comes from exercise, wears them out and debases their functions. Its action is just as sure and just as harmful as certain sorts of punishment, of falls and blows on the head, as morbid changes in the viscera and muscles. The result is that the child's mind and senses do not work clearly and in unison; his power of observation and right inference is dulled. This power is naturally of the greatest value, and when it does not exist in normally large amount, the results of its exercise are far from reliable.

There are other conditions which militate against the child in his efforts to understand and report what goes on about him. Among these are certain diseases of the eye, phenomena which occur in the end distribution of the optic nerve, among which are the light phenomena developed in the retina, the so-called light dust of the internal field of vision, shadowings and polychrome pictures. Moreover, these are conditions for which the adult, in ordinary sight, makes allowances, and so escapes deceit. But the child is easily enough led astray by processes in the retinal vessels, such as those involving the movements of the blood corpuscles, and pulsations of the central artery. Of course it is easy to understand the limitations attending opacities of the cornea and vitreous and all conditions producing entoptic shadows on the retina. But there are many other pathological conditions, for instance, such as catarrhs and irritations of the middle ear and irritations of the mucous membranes of the face and head, which, although not so direct, are just as potent to divert the course between impressions and their consequent expressions. One must distinctly keep in mind that this course is not necessarily direct, that an immature condition is the one best fitted to allow eccentric action, and that in order to obtain a true correspondence between concept and rightful expression, not only must the natural faculties be ordinarily well guarded and nourished, but also a certain fairly large amount of experience and practice is really essential. When this does not exist, one is very apt to find a disturbance of conception produced locally in the cortex of the brain, by which the child is unable to distinguish between the internal processes and their external conditions. If the ability to differentiate is impaired, an hallucination is present, dependent upon processes in those parts of the brain which preserve memory pictures of the most varied kinds.

One must distinctly keep in mind that such disorders, and others like them, are peculiarly apt to happen to children. The youthful organization, by the very fact of its immaturity, its unripe and unsettled conditions, invites them. Things which would affect an adult only slightly react upon a child in a startlingly acute and active manner. In a man a slight disturbance of the circulatory apparatus in the eye would, in all likelihood, be promptly recognized and discounted. In a child the false subjective impressions thus created would be regarded as real facts of objective importance. He could have no possibility or grounds of discrimination, and the opinions which would thus arise would naturally seem to him orderly and right. In the same way, any abnormal condition giving rise to abnormal sense-impressions or interruptions of normal connections in thought must make the child feel, see, and think things that are false. It is not hard to show that the consequences may be very serious. The main thing to keep in mind is that no ordinary child is a fit means to record and express accurate and truthful ideas. His main part in life is preparatory, constructive. He is being built up into a later creation that we call the adult. To measure him and his efforts by the standard of maturity is, speaking mildly, unwise. To put him in the responsible position of an adult is like placing a premium on miscarriages of justice.

The special environment which the child needs in his physical life has its analogue in the particular circumstances with which his mental life should be guarded. When the community gives him a greater responsibility than he is rightfully able to assume, it opens the door to disaster. The only safeguard that can effectually preserve the common interests is the withdrawal of such evidence from courts of law as a well-informed man must, *a priori*, doubt. The easiest solution of the matter would be to find some approximate age at which human beings are fairly close to a permanent standard which is in general reliable. At a glance one can see that nature has followed some such method, and has marked out the period which we call puberty as the boundary line. This demarcation would, of course, be not exact; but, at all events, it would be a nearer approach to a safe and conservative rule than any which we now have. In reality, there is at present no rule at all. Judges and lawyers vary according to the run of cases, by a sort of common sense, by a rule of thumb procedure.

Evidence that suits one is quite unsatisfactory to another, and both may be equally ignorant of real, scientific grounds for the acceptance or rejection of the testimony in question. The interest of all concerned lies in wiping out sources of permanent error.

CHAPTER VIII

THE DEVELOPMENT OF THE CHILD-CRIMINAL

IT has been truly said that every community has the government which it deserves; that it has the prevalence of order as far as its deserts go; and as truly one may say that every community has the juvenile criminals that it deserves, and deserves the juvenile criminals that prey upon it. For, in this respect, as in every other, there is no condition in a state that is caused by purely extraneous reasons. Such as it is, whether good or bad, it makes its own salvation. By its own constitution it is to be praised or blamed. In so far as it is worthy of triumphing over obstacles does it seek to find the reason for them, and with this quest comes the final solution. Thus problem after problem has been attacked, and the resulting triumphs have come after much struggling, much controversy, much seeking. The fights against slavery, against the oldtime habits of drinking, against the former methods in prison administration, have been long and bitter. Many a man has sought the truth in them, and has received misfortune, or even death, for his pains. But the world needed improvement, and deserved improvement, and a better condition came.

A somewhat analogous phase of development one may see in relation to the causation and treatment of the child-criminal. There is in the dim public mind an idea that we have not reached final conclusions in the matter; in fact, the subject of criminology, philosophically considered, is a comparatively new one. Some of the best minds have been working upon it, and even general attention has regarded it with the greatest interest. Each man who in the matter has shown ability, strengthened by thought and experience, has his special following of adherents, each of whom strives to bring a stone to help in building up the edifice begun by the master.

And the great number of varying ideas shows how far we are from a settlement of the case. Thus, Lombroso, one of the pioneers in criminology, has given a large place to the atavistic theory, that the criminal is a distinct type, that his special characteristics of mind and body come to him by the royal road of heredity. Dr. von Holder believes that example and poverty and lying are principal courses of crime. Garofalo disagrees, saying that criminal types are well fixed and constant, that "recidivation of the criminal is the rule, reformation the exception." What is more, perversity is a natural condition; in his mind education, religious and economic conditions are naught. Dr. Baer lays the blame in great part to the abuse of alcohol, and concludes that without such excesses the world would be immeasurably better. Richter, on the contrary, cries that alcoholics are light offenders; that serious crime is the result of epilepsy, of nervous irritations working in a fairly well known, but wrongly classified category. Prosper Despine lays greatest stress upon "moral blindness"; that cure is to come by moral elevation, not by prisons. Beranger supports him by the opinion that confirmed criminals are the effect of prisons, and is backed up by Dr. Laurent, who believes in the present system, but even more in its future development. Marimo and Gambara trace some connection between Wormian bones and vicious traits, but Corre finds nothing anatomically peculiar to criminals. Wines lays least stress upon theory, and cares least for it, claiming that "the principal hope of any material reduction in the volume of crime lies in its prevention rather than its cure."

At all events, we know that crime, although its cause is obscure, is a very present reality, and also, that on the whole it is increasing. Moreover, it is not hard to see that the relation between crime in general and juvenile crime is a constant one. They rise and fall together, and similar causes act in both for their development or repression. Factors of general life have the same effect upon both, and in addition, example and juxtaposition enable the old to lead the young. Therefore, when we say that practically no progress, by and large, has been made in diminishing the volume of crime, it is much the same as if we omit the word *crime*, and in its place substitute the phrase *juvenile crime*. Thus, in searching for a final reason in this matter, we may know that the two terms are interchangeable, and argument becomes much simpler.

Among other things, one is able to exclude from the ætiology certain factors which have often been blamed as the root of the evil. For instance, many people believe that a deficient education has the greatest tendency to brutalize and debase; that if intellectual enlightenment were more wisely spread, wrong-doing would of necessity shrink away. So common is this belief that anti-social acts committed by an ignorant man are often partially excused on the score of his ignorance, while equal wrong in an educated man is looked upon as showing far greater depravity, because he must have been sufficiently well instructed to know the nature of his acts. This may seem plausible enough, but it is far from being true. There is no inevitable relation between intellectual training and moral obliquity. The criminal is a criminal exactly the same whether he is stupid or instructed, the only difference being that in the latter case he is the more dangerous, on account of greater mental training. Moreover, there is no limit in education beyond which crime is impossible. On the other hand, one constantly finds instances of persons who, having received the benefits of good, or even the best, educational training, are nevertheless unable to act in an honest and upright manner. Besides this, one sees every day cases of wrong-doing committed by people whose intellectual advantages have been such that they, while possessing the ability to cloak the viciousness of their deeds, are able to act in an essentially criminal way. And it is only by means of their intellectual advantages that they continue with impunity so to act. This view, if one looks at the rather meagre statistics on the subject, is fully sustained. Those of Dr. Ogle are in point. In speaking of them he says: "Eighty-five per cent of the population were able to read and write in the years 1881–84, and as this represents an increase of ten per cent since the passing of the Elementary Education Act, it is probably not far from the mark to say that at the present time almost ninety per cent of the English population can read and write. In other words, only ten per cent of the population is wholly ignorant." This high percentage in instruction characterized a period that suffered from a large increase in crime, although the general relation between the two phenomena was not essentially different from that of other times. With the growth of statistical knowledge the truth of this is seen to have a wider and wider application.

Destitution, it is often said, is at the bottom of much of the crime in the world; that evil-doers are such because want crowds them out of the straight path of rectitude; that when poverty, with its sodden wings, overshadows a man, the light of truth and righteousness is shut out, and he becomes, to all intents and purposes, morally blind. This sounds very well when used, as it commonly is, to fill out begging letters. But as a matter of fact, it has not very much truth in it. Indeed, one finds, on examination, that the evidence is all the other way. Before looking at the testimony, one would naturally think that men who were oppressed by heavy burdens would be the most liable to lawbreaking, that by sheer force of desperation they would do anything to provide for the wants of to-day. Also, one would suppose that times of profound destitution would be most deeply marked with crime. The surprising thing is that both of these suppositions are false. One finds criminals, as a rule, to be those persons who have almost no responsible burdens, who in this respect are freest of all to use whatever faculties they may possess to the best advantage; and what is stranger still, one can easily ascertain that times of prosperity show the greatest flourishing of crime. Therefore, Morrison, a reliable writer, says: "It is a melancholy fact that the moment wages begin to rise, the statistics of crime almost immediately follow suit, and at no period are there more offences of all kinds against the person than when prosperity is at its height." In another place one reads: "It is found that the stress of economic conditions has very little to do with making these unhappy beings what they are; on the contrary, it is in periods of prosperity that they sink to the lowest depths." It is easy to collect such opinions, opinions which carry all the weight of authority with them. For the deeper investigators dig, and the nearer they come to the truth, the more clearly do their results agree. Therefore, one is prepared for a still later and very recent utterance which says: "When we begin to compare the distribution of pauperism with the distribution of crime, both juvenile and adult, it immediately becomes manifest that as a rule there is least pauperism where there is most crime, and of course least crime where there is most pauperism."

Many a man who has the interests of society close at heart may say that if ignorance is not the cause, if destitution is not the cause, then we have not far to search, for in drunkenness, which is ever with us, we have a reason whose validity is sure and certain. This seems very plausible, for the vicious and stupefying effects of the abuse of alcohol every one constantly witnesses. We so regularly see fortunes wrecked, careers blighted, men and women dragged down to the lowest depths by this vice, that it comes to represent everything bad. It is only a step farther to the conclusions that criminal impulses and acts must follow as the rightful sequel of it. This conclusion, while it flatters our sentimental side, is not based upon fact, and while the effects of inebriety are undoubtedly very bad, nevertheless, the causation of crime is not one of them. The real reason must lie somewhere else, as a study of statistical returns shows. We know that men in certain years of their life, between the ages of thirty and forty, are more liable than at any other time to become drunkards. Also, we know that at this time they are not most addicted to crime for which they may be indicted. We know that youths from sixteen to twenty-one years of age are most liable to commit such crimes, but on the other hand, they are not nearly so apt to be drunkards. When we come to juveniles less than sixteen years old, who may not in any way be said to be addicted to intoxication, we find that they produce indictable criminals in the proportion of two and sixty-one hundredths to every one thousand of the population of a similar age.

Compare this with the fact that among the older population of from thirty to forty years the proportion of indictable criminals is only two to one thousand. The conclusion is somewhat startling to preconceived ideas, but not more so than another comparison that is easily made. Men between thirty and forty years of age, as was said above, are much more liable to indulge in intoxicating excesses than at earlier periods of life; to put the matter more exactly, they are seven times more liable than at the period of life between sixteen and twenty-one years. On the other hand, in this latter period indictable crime is much more frequent, and, indeed, is more frequent than at any other time of life. Between these latter years there are three and three tenths convictions per annum for indictable crimes for every one thousand of the population. While at the age in which drunkenness is most found, there are only two and two tenths to an equal number. The difference of fifty per cent cannot be explained away so long as we hold to the conception that inebriety, whether in adults or children, is the cause of crime.

When one, in the search for this illusive cause, turns to heredity, the difficulty is just as great. This is in spite of the general belief that strongly marked traits must necessarily be the legacy of descent. The results of scientific investigation have, since 1859, been so startling, and the knowledge of them has been so perseveringly reiterated, that a really surprising amount of information on the subject has become diffused. One must of course expect that the applications of such knowledge should at times be inexact, and that is the very fact which experience illustrates. Because certain forms of insanity seem to leave an inherited taint, the general conclusion is frequently and very rashly reached that all forms of mental disease leave traces of a similar kind upon descendants. Because flowers produce flowers, because human beings beget human beings, the particular deduction is held that all individual traits may likewise be transmitted. In this way, an opinion in regard to crime is held, there is a general belief that the offspring of a man who has time and time again been convicted of anti-social acts must partake of his nature, must have an equally small amount of resistance to temptation, must be marked with the same convict's stripe, and at every possible opportunity attempts are made to trace such a connection. When, as the result of coincidence or of fact, the relationship has been established, the case is held up as a shining example of the popular belief. Our inquiry in this matter would be much simplified, and our faith in the broad working of heredity much more surely founded, if there were not so many evidences of an unjustly broad application of the principle in question. Our faith receives a crushing blow when we read in an authoritative English report that "in the five years, 1887–91, the children whose parents were habitual criminals formed two per cent of the industrial school (*i.e.*, youthful criminals) population." Another blow to this belief is the conclusion which a sifting of records forces upon one, that a criminal calling does not as a rule descend from father to son. On the other hand, in the vast majority of cases, the art is learned, not inherited. There seems to be need for a distinct training, which most children can easily absorb. Therefore, one is not at all shocked when a capable investigator enunciates the idea that crime "descends by apprenticeship, and not, as a rule, by parenthood."

There still remains the strong idea that acquired characteristics are not transmissible. We know that a parent who has suffered an amputation of a limb does not hand down to his children a like deformity; we know that in the pursuit of certain industries changes of form occur that are not transmitted, that in the cloth-cutting trade the distal phalanges of the left hand, on account of the pressure of holding the fabric, are twisted out of their normal lines, and finally constitute a permanent deformity. Although this deformity may exist in a man for a whole generation, nevertheless, his children do not bear any marks of it. A man may be exquisitely cultured, his children, under the proper circumstances, may be crude boors. It has not been proved that there is in human germ-plasm the faculty of absorbing the results of experience; all that can be demonstrated is the handing on of characteristics that are more nearly somatic. A certain shape of skull, a certain complexion, a certain dimension of stature, are clearly matters of inheritance. But characters which are produced by environment are not in the same category, are without the pale of hereditary influence.

Whatever effects are produced in this way are the result of a particular set of environments and do not necessarily extend beyond the person in whom they exist. Ordinary life is full of exemplifications of this which, with little trouble, may be clearly recognized. For instance, glance at the children committed to the industrial and reformatory schools in England. A short time ago, their numbers increased so markedly that the growth became the subject of official inquiry. The children were found to have followed not merely in the ordinary inheritable traits of their parents, but still more did they mirror the effects of their surroundings. They became criminals at their early age, because anti-social acts were the patterns upon which their lives were cast. Thus in the evidence brought out by the Royal Commission on Reformatory and Industrial Schools, a member of the Gateshead School Board deposed that the parents of the children committed to the Gateshead Industrial School consisted of the "refuse of the laborers in the large manufactories, men who have been thrown out of employment, and who have drifted into the very lowest class of the population."

On the other hand, to show how little effect heredity has in the production of juvenile crime, take the case of children, descended from approximately the same class of parents as those cited above, who were supported wholly or in part by London charity. According to the returns for the year 1891-92 of the Local Government Board, more than one-half of these children were taken care of without the parents being similarly provided for. As a condition of this support, the authorities held the power of carefully looking after their wards. They assiduously watched the ways of these children, they shut them off from the temptations and the vicious practices in which otherwise they must have participated, they stood, after a fashion, in the responsible position of parents. Restraint took the place of license, supervision came in where carelessness went out, responsibility was substituted for neglect. The result was truly remarkable, and the children, in consequence, seemingly lived quite different lives. So much changed were they that they were "hardly ever arrested as vagrants or thieves"; they were effectively shielded "from the very class of offences which come within the provisions of the Industrial School Acts." These facts serve as nails to hold the proof together, and in order to clinch them on the other side, it is necessary only to quote Morrison's generalization that "in the year 1891, forty-four per cent of the juveniles committed to reformatories were living at home, and had both parents alive." It must be quite clear that the home and its environment were the infecting material; the children served as culture media, and showed symptoms of infection, the principal of which was an anti-social tendency.

Of late years no study in the practical effects of heredity has carried with it a greater amount of popular belief than Dugdale's account of the "Jukes." They were a family of criminals and paupers whose history dates back to the first half of the eighteenth century. They lived together in a section of country which has been called "one of the crime-cradles of the State of New York." They were vicious, lazy, addicted to all manner of excess and crime. The total number of persons in this family and its descendants has been estimated at twelve hundred. Each generation handed on to the next all the crime and vice that the mind of man could possibly conceive. For the most part they herded together in roughly made shanties, where they lived a vile sort of life in common. With this place as a base of supplies, they preyed upon the community at large, distributing their evil influence in a way that is hard fully to realize. Generation after generation showed similar traits of disease, of viciousness, licentiousness and crime. An elaborate sociological study has been made of them, with the conclusion that the children were modeled after the parents. This family has pointed the moral in many discourses on heredity; they have served to fasten the idea in the minds of many people that in human beings the course of inheritance of characteristics is direct; that there is an inevitable fate which decides a child's mental and physical constitution, even before birth.

Such a conclusion is more than rash, and a fairly careful consideration of the facts will show how false it is. In this crowd of unfortunates there was no possibility of intercourse with decent citizens; the "Jukes" children were shut out from every humanizing influence; they were pariahs, constantly suspected, constantly distrusted, against whom the hand of every man was virtuously raised. Their children were born in the midst of the worst possible surroundings, and inhaled the odor of all manner of vice long before they knew what the boundaries between good and bad are. At a time when slavery was legal in this State, they showed how abysmal was their grade in the social scale by marrying mulattoes. With such surroundings any other fate was impossible. "The tendency of human beings is to obtain their living in the direction of least resistance, according to their views of what that direction is." With every example marking the way to crime, with every obstacle standing in the way to virtue, it would be almost miraculous if they were reputable. As the author himself has said, "want, bad company, neglect, form the environment that predisposes to larceny." When these factors are increased by all known means, one has a predisposition that becomes magnified into a salient trait.

Curiously enough, Dugdale has unconsciously given instances of the method by which the viciousness of the "Jukes" might have been prevented, by which these seemingly hopeless characters might have been reclaimed. He mentions a married pair of this family who removed from the rest to where they were not so well known. Naturally, the outlook changed, they left the ranks of beasts, and took their stand among human beings. Their offspring developed in much the same way as the other children of the new neighborhood, as many children of a fairly respectable parentage. As the author says: "This pair thus measurably protected themselves and their progeny from the environment of eight contaminating persons, all immediate relatives, whose lives were, with few exceptions, quite profligate." He mentions still another case that is equally instructive. One of the "Juke" women, a harlot and criminal, died in the poor house, leaving a daughter of the age of one year behind her. This child, according to hard ideas of heredity, should have year by year shown increasing tendencies toward evil ways, and in all likelihood, if she had remained within the taint of her family's influence, she must have done so; but fortunately, a lady of wealth adopted her, gave her some of the care which she needed, and at the time of the report — when she was old enough, according to the family standard, to show vicious tendencies — she was seemingly quite normal. If this happy change in her fortunes had not occurred, if she had remained with her mother's family, "which must have been sufficient without heredity to stimulate licentious practices," there is very little doubt of what her fate would have been. And then there would have been still another case of the inexorable law by which the attributes of the parents show themselves in the children. In similar ways it would be easy to multiply such instances in other families, where children of vicious birth, when adopted into finer surroundings, blossomed out into useful men and women, and in like manner, one can find enough cases of well-born offspring degenerating far below their natural plane, when their atmosphere was such as to make the falling off logical.

If now we are not satisfied with heredity as the essential cause of crime, if ignorance, if destitution, if drunkenness, are not the cause, can we turn with greater faith to the other explanations? To most of them, certainly not. For these are such as have too little weight, which at most may be called secondary. Various authors have claimed that climate is a controlling cause, that variations in latitude have important significance. But this can hardly be the fact, for all climates and lands have similar crimes and anti-social acts; they all seem to suffer from the same sickness, and all are powerless to heal themselves. It is true that there may be some difference in the symptoms, such as the greater proportion of crimes against the person in Southern countries, and the greater proportion of offences against property in Northern. But the disease is to all intents and purposes the same the world over. Seasons, others say, are responsible. Here again one is dissatisfied, for there is no season which is without its wrong deeds, nor is there even the satisfaction of logical sequence between the exigencies of the weather, and the showing which crime makes. Thus one would expect that in the harshest seasons, when human needs are greatest, when want is most keenly felt, men would become so desperate as to throw aside social restraints, and in order to satisfy their wants, prey upon whoever came into their hands. But as a matter of fact, all this is quite different from the real state of things. Surprising as it may seem, nevertheless it is true, that crime is commonest in the pleasantest seasons of the year, when people have least in nature to contend with, when they are most abroad and mingling together. It has even been said that food is the acting cause, that strong meat foods inflame the passions, heat the blood, and incline men to deeds of violence. This is so far from the truth that it needs merely the mention of a concrete case to set it at rest. The Italians as a people have a largely vegetable diet that is not as "heating," their food is not nearly as "strong" as that of the people of the United States. Nevertheless, the percentage of crime among the Italians is among the highest, while that of the United States is among the low. Another case in point is that of the native inhabitants of India, whose diet is both light and meagre. And yet, if it were not for the interference of the carnivorous English, they would even now be addicted to the almost universal practice of infanticide.

In ruling out these factors of poverty, ignorance, inebriety, heredity, food and weather, we have done something to clear the view, and have brought a decision within reasonable distance. We may be helped by reading the results of investigations in the subject, no matter where conducted. Thus we know positively that crime occurs in all ranks and at all ages, that the particular form which it assumes depends upon the maturity and circumstances of the individual. A child of seven years is unable on account of his immaturity to commit highway robbery, or most of the offences against the person; he is so weak in mind and body that the most he can do is to be guilty of vagrancy or larceny. Any boy, for instance, who is well cared for, who is well nourished and lovingly watched, is plainly unable to fall into this category. Such offenders one would not find among the offspring of the well-to-do and more fortunate classes. On the contrary, among those people whose parental care is least, whose ability and willingness to attend to the needs of their children are smallest, one should find the greatest numbers of this sort of delinquents. Such a class one finds in the lowest grade of workers, among the so-called general laborers, for their ranks are in large part made up of men who have failed in other branches, men who have almost no training of mind or body worthy of the name, men who are least self-controlled, least provided with the means of supplying the needs of a family. They have the greatest difficulty in maintaining a respectable position in society; their short-sightedness and improvidence prevent them from seeing the consequences of their acts, and naturally they easily fall victims to their wants or their passions. This is the reason why low-skilled workers are proportionately from three to four times more numerous in prisons than in the general community. It follows, consequently, that their children are least provided for, that they have the worst examples set before them, that they are most liable to contract vicious practices. Thus it has been officially reported that "of the number of young offenders committed to reformatories in the year 1891, there were, as near as it is possible to calculate, thirty-two per cent descended on one or both sides from parents who neglected to control them, or deserted them, or were in prison for crime." Here one sees a direct connection of cause and effect; these children were vicious, not necessarily because their parents were ignorant or poor, but simply because, since worthy examples to imitate were absent, and opportunities to wrong-doing meant gratification, they took the easiest road to satisfy their wants.

Even after they have committed wrong, have been

caught and punished, they are no whit improved.
They are released from prison more thoroughly than
ever infected with viciousness by companionship with
a herd of youthful offenders — imps, one might call
them; they return to their homes and former surroundings, and the same old story repeats itself. The
only change consists in their greater age, their wider
experience, their broader possibilities for mischief. It
is inevitable that their ways should be as bad as before
or worse, so that one is not surprised, when reading
the returns for the year 1894, to learn that sixty-four
per cent of the offenders who had been committed to
reformatories had been convicted of crime two or more
times. It must be so, and any other result would be
illogical. The whole train of causes leads up to this
fact. Other elements in the causation of crime have a
similar working. Although drunkenness is in itself no
real cause, and although children, vicious or otherwise,
are not as a rule given to drink, nevertheless, inebriety
helps to make the environment from which young criminals go forth. The offspring of drunken parents are
neglected, are demoralized by the example and the condition of their parents. They are left without care and
support at a time when these things are as necessary
as air and food. And naturally enough, they pick up
their living in the manner of least resistance. This
must surely lead them to the dock; it accounts for the
estimate that from fifteen to twenty per cent of youth-

ful convicts are descended from parents who are usually termed drunkards. Here again we must keep in mind that alcohol has no wondrous and special working of its own that is worse than any other agency. It is no worse in its results than certain other factors, the abuse of which leads to unsettling the mind and body. In the majority of cases such general abuses are at work. A clear view of the physiological development of the child would *a priori* convince one of this truth. But the proof is made strong when one reads that "at least eighty in every hundred of parents of young criminals are addicted to vicious, if not criminal, habits."

It is not in mind and disposition alone that children, by growing up in circumstances of neglect and chance, are affected. Their bodies at the same time, and in somewhat similar ways, are retarded. Naturally these two effects must act upon each other, making abnormal growth still more pronounced. Thus children come to have weak bodies, not so much from heredity as from their manner of life, not because they were born so, but because their environment kept them down. One may see how true this is by consulting the published report of the Committee of the British Association of 1883, in regard to the relative statures of boys between the ages of eleven and twenty-two in the population at large, and in that of the industrial and reformatory schools. They found the tallest boys, in proportion to their age, in the public schools; below them came the boys in the so-called middle-class schools; then those in the elementary schools and in private military schools; and, last of all, the inmates of the industrial schools. A still more sweeping report was made by another Committee, which stated that the industrial schools showed a greater percentage of unnaturally small children than any other class in the whole English population. These statements are rendered much more vivid by knowing that in the various planes mentioned above there was a difference of six inches in stature between the first and the last. These facts are pregnant with meaning, and the better the evidence on the subject, the more positive are results. Still another Committee, the Anthropometric Committee of the British Association, in the same year made similar researches in regard to variations in weight. Their results both for boys and girls coincided most closely with those cited above. At any age between six and sixteen the children of the industrial schools are far below the average in weight, while between these children and those of the population at large there was, at the age of fourteen years, a difference of twenty-four and three-fourths pounds. When one realizes the close relationship between body and mind, — a relationship so intimate that no man can say where it begins and ends, — one can see the full importance of these figures. Dwarfed bodies, as a rule, mean dwarfed minds and souls, poorly nourished frames do not go hand in hand with a clear and normal intellectual and moral growth. What helps one helps the other; what twists and weakens one helps to debase and enfeeble the other. Practical illustrations of this may be seen in Dr. Warner's researches, which state that about one-third of all youthful criminals have a defective mental development. From my own experience, which has been fairly large, I believe that this figure underrates, rather than overrates, the fact.

It should be clearly understood that the causation, as well as the management of pauperism, vice and crime, stands upon a foundation of physiology and anatomy, rather than unstable metaphysics and emotions. Such conditions exist in accordance with definite laws of development; they act just as steadily and ruthlessly as the laws of gravitation, of the conservation of energy. One of the troubles in considering the matter is that undue stress has been put upon heredity. Claims have been made for it, and phenomena have been referred to it that rightly belong in other categories. This idea has been so used that it serves as a scapegoat, freeing parents, guardians and the community from a responsibility which rightfully rests upon them. When a child, oppressed by hidden or open disease, by ignorance and neglect, by faulty systems of training, shows naturally unfavorable characteristics, the guilt is promptly laid at the convenient door of hereditary descent. He is supposed to be bad because some of his ancestors failed to react in normal ways to the *stimuli* of their environment; the signs of viciousness in his life, because his mother or grandmother, laboring possibly under the stress of thoughtlessness, ignorance, or lack of controlling influences, acted in a manner that society does not consider right or feasible, are construed to indicate an irradicable depravity of temperament. The very same impulses, or the characteristics from which they spring, may, under different auspices, be quite easily understood, and quite as easily accounted for.

The exigencies of modern civilization are quite artificial and carry with them their special changes in the organism. Such changes must be certainly felt in the cerebral tissue, and once felt, the person in his ordinary life, obeying the call of such acquired characteristics, acts in a direct and logical way, without regard to where that way may lead him. A cure for an uneven development lies not in punishment, imprisonment, or ostracism, — all of which are bound to make the development still more uneven, — but in methods which will tend to abolish these artificial disabilities, which will promote a normal rounding out of cerebral growth, even though generations of effort are needed to provide a cumulative force that will be sufficient to overcome the effect of centuries of wrong ideas and faulty methods. A withered limb is thought to be lightly regained if treatment for a period many times the length of the original pathological process is finally successful. And there is no inherent reason why a greater patience and hopefulness should not be used where the nutrition of the nervous system is concerned.

That this question of nutrition lies at the very base of the problem there is the best reason to believe; that arrested development is at the bottom of mental incapacity we know for a certainty. By a parity of reasoning and experience, the opinion that it is of equal importance in the formation of character must likewise be held. Children are not born moral, do not become cultured and educated by a heaven-sent gift of intuition. Besides this, there is very little of spontaneous endowment in the matter. The process is one of gradual up-building, of an unfolding of cerebral cells. It begins with the very beginning of the being, at the moment of conception, and ends—no one knows exactly where. Disturbances of nutrition occur in obedience to known as well as unknown causes. Those which result in physical deformities leave their mark so plainly that they have been freely discussed. On the other hand, mental and psychical impressions may be made in an exactly similar way. They produce deformities quite as frequently, although they may not be designated by this name. According to manner of occurrence, time, duration or social position, they may be called eccentricity, crime, weakness, rashness, or any of the other terms which we give to unusual characteristics. When one realizes that nutrition means all the circumstances of life which affect tissue change, one comes to feel that no influence is entirely outside of its limits. Wrong methods of feeding, of rest, of amusements, of ordered attention, of occupation, are some of the elements which help to make a child one-sided. As he grows older the opportunities for divergence in his development increase in large degree. With increasing activity he is more and more allowed to follow in his own feebly directed desires, there is less and less of principle and a correspondingly greater amount of expediency in his training. These things, as we know, diminish his power of physical resistance in direct ratio to the extent of their prevalence. When one reads that "from childhood up to manhood the delinquent population loses a higher proportion of its numbers than the juvenile population as a whole," one has the statement of facts in gross, but the principle back of it applies to every child in the community. While it is true that the abuses in question are greatest in quantity and quality among the most unfavorable portion of people, nevertheless, they are scattered in varying frequency in practically all circles, and their results are in like manner discriminated.

As Dugdale most wisely said, "Environment is the ultimate controlling factor in determining careers." For environment is the steady source of sense-impressions which, if repeated sufficiently often, produce permanent states of mind. Of course there are many cases of a congenital condition of varying development in function and nutrition. And where the surroundings of the child are not of the wisest, these aberrations become still more exaggerated. It is in such cases that there is most need to find out not only what variations are present, but also to arrange every influence that comes in contact with him to the end of making the balance of faculties even. It is not in the lowest classes alone that such disproportions exist, nor are the limits of viciousness necessarily bound to those of indictable crime. In every grade of life one finds the best evidence of inharmonious growth. The wealthy rake, the intellectual crank, the heartless egoist, the useless idler, are all subjects of the disease of disproportion in cerebral development. The symptoms vary according to the particular combination of nerve cells and the environment in which the person has lived. The criminal's course is biologically, although not forensically, similar. In most cases there is no inherent reason why he should be markedly vicious. Naturally this statement does not include the cases, which unquestionably occur at times, of a seemingly spontaneous viciousness, a congenital moral blindness, a crime-tendency by intuition. Although such cases are rare, nevertheless, their existence may not be denied. In the same way, physicians occasionally see cases of antenatal deformity, babies born without limbs, or eyes, or any other portion of the body. The occurrence of these pitiful curiosities does not invalidate the fact that the vast majority of losses of limbs and eyes is due to known, observed and preventable causes. It requires no argument to prove that preventable disasters throw upon the responsible guardian a heavy burden of guilt. In similar ways one may show that the person with a deformed and maimed character has not himself alone to blame for the misfortune.

It is a regrettable fact that one does not often find families where the best provision is made against preventable disasters in character. What children see and hear, whether it be good or bad, they will imitate. They learn the lessons of their life not so much from books, sermons or lectures, as from practical demonstration. A household which is characterized by vicious habits of mind and body brings forth a brood of children that are fit to hold the community as their proper prey. Year by year, as example makes a progressively stronger impress, they become more inclined to harmful lives and ideals. It is for this reason that one finds offences increasing as maturity approaches. Any species of training is more thoroughly absorbed by a child of seven years than one of five years. By the age of sixteen, he is not only more capable of action, but also his mental processes are more thoroughly crystallized. When he reaches maturity only a moral revolution can change his ways of thinking and acting. In the ordinary family circle an analogous process is constantly working : ideals of speech, of demeanor, of morals, are absorbed just as surely as dry sand sucks up water. The child represents in his future growth what his imitative faculty has fed upon. If he has lived where deceit is practised, where courtesy is an article of luxury, where metaphorically speaking people go about in their moral slippers, where above all he notices that one code of conduct is practised at home while quite another is publicly advocated, he is quite unable to realize in his later self a high standard of ethical bearing.

A parent has more to do than merely provide for his child's physical wants and his educational needs as regulated by state limitations; indeed, these things are not the most important. In addition he should feel himself bound to set a model and provide an atmosphere that stands for the best ideal which he is able to conceive. The training consists not so much in formal expositions of duty as in the daily practice, the hourly practice, of them. He is bound to feel that he has in himself the powers and the responsibilities of a maker, a creator. Every faculty and every possibility in him he must regard as glorified, because from them may start streams of moral energy which are bound to increase with their duration in time. Such doctrine has often been looked upon as proper to the pulpit; and it may be, but simply in the measure that all right conduct should be similarly treated. Outside of this, however, so long as it is founded upon known principles of psychological growth, it has a real bearing upon the proper training and treatment of children in everyday life, it has a definite biological importance. There is as much need for the expert in pediatrics to include it in a scheme for the bringing up of children as there is to work out the need for a proper method of feeding, a proper care of the eyes, or any subject involving a right ordering of the physical economy.

One of the most revered East Indian theologies has an article of its teaching which inculcates the idea of a permeating individual responsibility in every phase of life. It holds that no word, no thought, no act,— in short, no circumstance in life, no matter how minute and trivial it may be,— but has its definite share in making up the sum of existence. That the characteristic results are not immediately apparent is no reason for losing sight of the antecedent causes, any more than one should be sceptical about the origin of electrical manifestations because the generating cause cannot be seen. Human senses are gross, and human reason, in most cases, is not over- fine; and a dependence upon their spontaneous coöperation and approbation is too often unreliable. We are apt to grasp at generalizations with which we have become familiar and to consider that outside of this there is no truth. Thus, for instance, by constant iteration we have come to believe that various social evils are caused by crowding many inhabitants into a comparatively small space. We forget the very important fact that, in the main, evil results start from this condition only in the presence of industrial and economic instability. It is, on the other hand, unquestionably true that a crowded population living in economic and industrial stability is much better than a sparse one in equally uncertain conditions. The same principle may be applied all through life to the main question of culpability: children, as a rule, act out in their lives the influences which have been brought to bear upon them. Their natural faculties are modifiable and are modified by their environment to such an extent that, in the main, responsibility for their careers is largely due to the influences in which they have spent the most plastic years of their life.

CHAPTER IX

The Child's Development as a Factor in Producing the Genius or the Defective

THE study of biology brings with it a knowledge of the fact that animal life, in its various orders and species, develops unevenly, that the fruition of this development — useful and matured action — grows in ways that are peculiar to each kind. Moreover, we know, as has been stated in an earlier part of this work, that the higher the organism the longer does it require to attain a full development of its capabilities.

So low a form as *amœba* comes into existence and attains full organic and functional maturity at the same time. As one ascends in the scale of life, one finds not only a progressively longer period between birth and maturity, but also a progressively greater interval between organic and functional growth. As Clouston puts it: "The difference between what the brain of a child of eight and the brain of a man of twenty-five can do and can resist is quite indescribable. The organ at these two periods might belong to two different species of animals so far as its essential qualities go." At a glance one can see how important in regulating one's ideas of growth this rule is, but the whole story is not yet stated. Even after the main necessities of organic form exist, a long time is required before the active and efficient working power comes into play. The biologist is deeply impressed by the remarkable fact that the nerve cell requires a long time, even after it reaches its full bulk, to grow into the full exercise of its ultimate powers. "We may say that after most of the nerve cells of the brain have attained their proper shape and size, it takes them the enormous time of eighteen or nineteen years to attain such functional perfection as they are to arrive at."

One must keep in mind that the main business of a nerve cell is to elaborate energy. This process is the result of chemical decomposition of cell contents, a result which constitutes in part the phenomenon of physiological metabolism. In so far as this metabolism is normal and healthful, energy is stored up, which expresses itself in ways that are characteristic of the cell activities. The quantity of energy to be disposed of does not necessarily depend upon the quantity of waste or decomposition in the cell. Indeed, one regularly finds a progressively great amount in proportion to the immaturity of the acting cells. In the cortical cells of the infant or the defective person of greater age (whose condition approximates to that of the infant) one finds a comparatively large production of chemical metabolism. Such cells are thus in a condition of natural instability which for very small causes assumes a phase of irritability; this is commonly out of all proportion to the exciting cause. In such a way pathological action is easy of occurrence and may be really serious in results. It is difficult enough for these cells to work normally, to make and direct sufficient energy to respond to normal impulses in normal ways; and on account of this difficulty, abnormal and pathological development or arrest of development is and ought to be correspondingly easy.

This is true not only theoretically but also practically; and one can see proofs of it in any clinic for nervous diseases. As Sachs says: "During the period of incomplete development the nervous system responds much more energetically to morbid influences than it does in later years." As the nervous system grows older and attains a greater degree of functional independence, the amount of energy produced is more directly in ratio with the amount of chemical change. Likewise, we know that chemical decomposition can come about only when there is a sufficiently large supply of material to work upon. This material must be constantly renewed through the regular channels of nourishment, of assimilating convertible substances which are able to supply the needs of the cell. There-

P

fore one would expect greater energy, other things being equal, from a well fed cell and less energy from a poorly fed one. So far as this view is concerned, it makes little difference whether the cell in question is nourished equally with other cells or whether it absorbs nutrition at the expense of, and to the exclusion of, other cells. In the first case, there would be a general ability to elaborate characteristic energy, in the second there would be a disproportionate, a one-sided development. The first would have greater all-round growth, the second would have a smaller growth or an atrophy in one part with a greater growth or hypertrophy in another.

Another function of nerve cells is that of discharging the energy stored up. When each cell or group of cells discharges its force in a manner that carries out the special reason for its existence, we have as a result the normal and ordinary working of all the parts of the body. When one group of cells discharges a greater amount of energy than its normal share, a lack of balance results which shows itself, as a rule, throughout the whole organism. Thus we know that the action of the heart is heightened by the so-called accelerator nerves and lowered by the so-called depressor nerves or nerve cells. These two sets, by their harmonious interaction, regulate the work of the heart muscle so that it adjusts itself easily to all the varying changes of blood pressure, heat dissipation, and all the other multiform physiological phenomena that properly belong to it. If in consequence of the over-nutrition of one group, or too great a discharge of energy, the balance of developmental power is not maintained, there must come about a deviation from normal work and nutrition, with characteristic symptoms of the disorder.

The same idea holds good in all matters of control, whether reflex, automatic, or voluntary. And in exactly the same way that muscular action and muscular tone are controlled, just so the parts of the nervous system, which by their exercise supply thought, work out their purpose. Every part of this system is subject to these same laws, so that there can be no difference in the elaboration of energy no matter what its ultimate mode of expression may be. Thus the cells whose energy goes towards providing the basis for the moral thought of a man, are subject to the same laws as those which provide the basis of the more exclusively intellectual processes. Considerations which encourage or discourage one affect the other in like manner.

There is another fact to be kept in mind, and it concerns the fact of systematic inhibition. All through the central nervous system there are cells and groups of cells which have the function of retarding and blunting the more positive energy developed by others, and in certain cells of a high type both negative and positive functions are present. Thus we find that all through the nervous tissue there run series of counterchecking influences, whose nice equilibrium means fine adjustment of potentiality. When one factor or another is out of proportion, a one-sided action must result. Also we find that the restraining or inhibitory function is the last to develop. This is chronologically correct, for a restraining force has no reason for its existence until the energy which it is meant to restrain is really present. In the same logical chronology we find that the vital automatic processes, heart and lungs, have their inhibitory force ready to act approximately well at birth; the various somatic reflexes blossom out in their turn, while the more clearly intellectual are the last of all to come to maturity. In childhood disturbances of inhibition are oftenest found, and likewise, for this reason, one finds in childhood a great tendency to neurotic action, which works in the way of making the abnormal child. Even when the centres of these reflexes have attained their approximate form, their energy is discharged more easily, more irregularly, more capriciously, than in the adult. When the environment, the general nutrition, of the child is imperfect, the instability of the nervous state is increased, and abnormal action is more likely. Such abnormal action, as was mentioned above, may consist in a general weakness, a partial weakness, or a partial weakness associated with a partial overgrowth. All three conditions are unfortunate, for they mean limited possibilities in accomplishing the full objects of life.

This much one must have clearly in mind when considering the defective and the genius among children. Then one gradually comes to see that there is no sharp line between them, that there is a bourne where the dull black of idiocy and the brilliant white of unusually great mental power meet and blend in the quiet gray of the commonplace. As Seguin says, idiocy is "an infirmity of the nervous system which has for its effect the abstraction of the whole or part of the organs and the faculties of the child from the normal action of the will." This abstraction comes as the result of arrested development, of insufficient nutrition, and should not be looked upon as an inevitable and immovable thing which occurs regularly in the course of descent, like curly hair, or full stature, or like certain specific diseases. The more one sees of defective children, the more one is impressed with the striking fact that physical elements play an important part in the production and continuance of psychical and intellectual impotence. Given certain impaired cells, and the equilibrium of cells throughout the body is shaken. Given a tuberculous condition, the most common disability with which unfortunates have to contend, and the chances of good mental growth are greatly lessened.

The effects of such a condition are so marked that Shuttleworth, as the result of experience for a quarter of a century with defective children, says: "A phthisical family history is, indeed, a predominant factor traceable in our cases, the percentage in which this was found being twenty-eight and thirty-one hundredths, against twenty-one and twenty-eight hundredths in which hereditary mental weakness (insanity or imbecility) was recorded." Again, Dr. Ireland states that "perhaps two-thirds, or even more, of all idiots are of the scrofulous constitution." Tuberculosis acts in this way not because it has an especial relation to mental weakness, but merely because it undermines and wears out the general physical constitution. The resulting condition is one of lowered nutrition, which affects every cell in the body. On the other hand, where, in the presence of a tuberculous predisposition, adequate means of controlling the diathesis are used, there is every reason to believe that not only will the general condition be kept at a normal standard, but also the tendency to impaired intellectual power will be checked. The two things have the close relation of cause and effect, and cannot well be separated.

With increasing experience with these cases, one sees more and more reason for believing in a lack of nutrition as the ultimate cause of defective mental growth. In an analysis of English cases, fully thirty per cent were attributed to ill-health in the mother, to injuries, to accidents, to shock during the period of gestation, all of which may be regarded as means of lowering vitality in the offspring. This is one-half again as much as were caused by an epileptic and neurotic descent, where there might be ground for a belief in an hereditary predisposition or transmission. I regard this belief as problematical, for there are the best of reasons for holding that neurotic and epileptic conditions stand for impoverished nervous conditions, whether they are joined to equally poor somatic states or not. So long as this is the case, the progeny of persons so constituted could not be expected to be strong. Here again there is the rigid relation of cause and effect.

Some of the familiar causes are most to be respected for their age, rather than their strict conformity with ascertained truth. For instance, there is a common belief that consanguinity of parents is a potent factor in the causality of idiocy and allied conditions. But in the analysis of English cases referred to, less than five per cent seem to be capable of such a classification. And even in this small percentage, the main tendency which one can see is a risk of intensifying family weaknesses. Another time-honored cause — intemperance in the parents — seems to be responsible for only about sixteen per cent of the whole number. And in this case, again, one has to decide whether the intemperance itself was the real cause, or whether the lowered vitality which preceded, accompanied, or followed the excess, should be blamed. In the latter case, the decision would once more rest with the fact of impaired nutrition as the primal cause; and intemperance would take its place with a multitude of other factors as merely a means for inducing cytoplasmic poverty. Therefore, one is not at all surprised in reading an authoritative opinion to this effect: "Not every drunken parent procreates an idiot; but when inherited nervous instability from this or other causes is intensified in the next generation by injudicious marriage, or by unfavorable environment, instances of mental degeneracy are apt to occur."

Even in so low a condition as microcephalus, — a state so low as to have simian and even theroid resemblances, — the only cause that one can find is something which lowers the vital nutrition of the child before birth. Whether it is the general health and strength of the mother, or the wise conduct of her everyday life, whether it inheres in some nervous shock or the strain from physical exhaustion, is very hard to say. At all events, we know that the condition does not necessarily follow any broad path of heredity; and on the other hand we are quite as sure that any of the alternatives mentioned above, as well as other causes working in similar ways, must be at the root of the trouble. The question of responsibility and the possibility of avoiding this blight is one that naturally springs into the mind. But I prefer to leave it undiscussed, at least for the present. The main fact, however, is to recognize that mental defects are due to poor work in the making and the rearing of cell tissue, that they are of varying degree according to the severity of the causes at work, and that the differences between them are differences in degree rather than of kind. Likewise, it is well known that the injury may not be a general one; for every observer has noticed that certain parts of the cerebral tissue may be of lower development or vitality than others, and that the location of the vicious development comes about according to events of which we may be ignorant.

Even in the lowest grade of human beings one finds at times a surprising keenness and activity in certain parts of the brain, while the remaining portions may be remarkably crude. Thus Seguin describes "idiots who discriminated species of woods and stones merely by smell without having recourse to sight"; at the same time the other senses were very obtuse and unequal. Ascending somewhat higher in the scale, one might instance such cases as that of very low savages, as for example the African Bushmen, whose intellectual development is exceedingly small, but who, on the other hand, have a special gift in hearing or smell that is truly wonderful. Or, one might take such striking cases as that of Blind Tom, a negro, born of common slaves, whose general mentality was that of an idiot, but whose musical gifts were so extraordinary as to entrance thousands of people who heard him. Or, again, one might mention the German "Lightning Calculator," Dase, who possessed very wonderful mathematical faculties joined with a general intellectual development that was pitiably meagre. Such cases exist in striking numbers. They fortify the opinion that intellectual power is, seemingly, distributed vicariously, that good and bad, high or low, may go together, that intentional or unintentional disadvantages will lower the nutrition, and so the function of any part; while conversely, intentional or unintentional advantages will heighten both nutrition and function.

There is still another fact of great importance, that one should keep in mind. It is the possibility of improving a defective mental condition by the various means that will provide strength for the weakened tissue, that will nourish starved cells, that will awaken the parts which sleep in what seems to be a death-like slumber. The means for doing this are gradually becoming known, and with this greater knowledge better results are obtained. A strong indication of what may be done is given by the improvement which comes with the change from bad to good sanitary surroundings. When so elementary a matter as proper sanitation can change a defective to a higher order of person, a world of light is by implication thrown upon the subject of intellectual growth. That such a change can be accomplished there can be no doubt; for we have as testimony the work of Geggenbühl and his remarkable success in treating cretins by a change of surroundings. The unfortunate creatures, who in the dull and shadowed valleys of the Alps were but little better than beasts, became vastly improved, vastly higher in general capabilities when removed to the bracing air, the generous sunshine and the exhilarating freedom of the Abendberg. In the same way that weakened lungs, feeble muscles, shrunken limbs may be helped, brain tissue may be improved organically and functionally. Moreover, possible improvement is not confined to any special part of the organism. Any tissue, no matter at what stage the developmental impulse has been arrested, may under proper environment be made to take on an added growth and a stronger vitality. When Seguin was Director of the Asylum for idiots at Bicêtre, he wrote a report of his experience that was not only interesting, but also deeply instructive. "Idiots," he said, "have been improved, educated, and even cured; not one in a thousand has been entirely refractory to treatment; not one in a hundred who has not been made more happy and healthy; more than thirty per cent have been taught to conform to moral and social law, and rendered capable of order, of good feeling, and of working like the third of a man; more than forty per cent have become capable of the ordinary transactions of life under friendly control, of understanding moral and social abstractions, of working like two-thirds of a man; and twenty-five to thirty per cent have come nearer and nearer the standard of manhood, till some of them will defy the scrutiny of good judges when compared with ordinary young men and women."

All this constitutes a marvellous change from the time when Howard in plain terms pilloried the shocking customs that existed in prisons and asylums. Such institutions then were veritable plague-spots of vice, misery, inhuman cruelty. Low mental conditions became still lower, the defective was regarded as a wild beast whose proper care, because his condition was considered permanent and incapable of improvement, consisted in annihilating and crushing subjection. More than one man in going from one of these cages to another traveled on horseback, that his clothes might lose the stench with which they were impregnated. Physical abuses and degeneration went hand in hand with mental. And the creature who was cursed with a palpable psychical infirmity would have been more fortunate to have lived in the rigorous days of Lacedæmon when such as he were summarily killed off. Nevertheless, the customs and opinions of a century ago have not been quite stamped out. The general public still feel the inertia of by-gone ideas. They still regard the defective as a being who is comparable to a man born without limbs and without all necessary viscera, whose state is fixed as that of a lightning-blasted tree or a bare and sterile rock. They do not keep in mind that in speaking of the feeble-minded they must include, as Dr. Firnald does, "all degrees and types of congenital defect, from that of the simply backward boy or girl, but little below the normal standard of intelligence, to the profound idiot, a helpless, speechless, disgusting burden, with every degree of deficiency between these extremes." They do not understand that there can be no clear line of division between these classes, and that since there is no such line there must consequently be the possibility of developing and reclaiming all in some varying degree, so long as there is a possible improvement in any.

The natural conclusion, then, is that the various means of improvement, whether ante- or post- natal, are adventitious, are with growing knowledge capable of control. Even the degree of reclamation is not fixed, the limit of yesterday being found to-day quite inadequate to mark off the extremes of possibility. When one reads in the last national census that there were in the United States in 1890, nearly one hundred thousand "idiotic and feeble-minded persons," that "taking the country as a whole, there are two feeble-minded persons to every thousand persons," one is well-nigh overwhelmed by this burden of helpless misery, inefficiency and misfortune that might in some degree be avoided. There can be no doubt that a beginning in solving the problem has been made, although it is nothing more than a beginning. One begins to have hope when one reads in the first report of the trustees of the State Asylum at Syracuse: "At the base of all our efforts lies the principle that, as a rule, none of the faculties are (is) absolutely wanting, but dormant, undeveloped, and imperfect." And the hope is continued when one reads the two rules promulgated at Bicêtre: "To exercise the imperfect organs so as to develop their functions," and "To train the functions so as to develop the imperfect organs."

If, then, no line between degrees of mental deficiency may be drawn, if, moreover, the deficiency may, on account either of invigorating environment or natural endowment, be so slight that there is no appreciable difference between it and the general average of intelligence, then it follows that the so-called normal state cannot be sharply marked off, and is indeed incapable of sharp definition. All that one means by the phrase, "average" or "normal," is, on the one hand, the possession of a general amount of cellular nutrition by which the person is able to do sufficient work to support himself, as well as to absorb sufficient discipline to make himself a bearable member of the society in which he lives; on the other hand, the definition goes so far as to include a well-rounded and able-bodied intellectual impulse that enables the possessor to make a definite and respected place for himself in the world. Between these extremes there are very many grades, and men ascend or descend from one to another slowly, but nevertheless with a fair amount of ease. The character of their environment goes very far to lay out the paths which they are to follow. For the large majority of people are endowed in their mental constitutions very much as in their physical; they have sufficient nutritional activity to carry out the demands of the life in which they have grown up, and not much besides. In this way one can understand how it is that but few men can possibly be ahead of their time, how a fact which seems so simple as to be almost trivial would to our ancestors have appeared as a wild flight of the imagination. An ordinary school-boy of to-day absorbs with ease knowledge which would have been exceedingly difficult for an Elizabethan to acquire. Physical phenomena upon which the use of steam and electricity are based, ideas which underlie freedom and universal suffrage, theories of art and religion, which would have been almost impossible for the seventeenth or eighteenth century man, are readily assimilated by the ordinary student of our high schools.

Through all the past years there has been a slow but steady growth of nerve and body tissues. In addition cerebral cells have become used to receiving added and new impressions, the associational centres have had a great amount of exercise, the capacity for work, for assimilation, has been largely increased. In the face of these facts the fear, which one frequently hears expressed about the sum of human knowledge and experience being so enormous that we are close on to the limit of acquisition, is plainly futile. It is true that the world's circumstances have greatly enlarged, but the growth has on the whole been so gradual, has had so many preparatory stages ranging over a great length of time and, besides, has followed so inevitable a path, that the idea of overstrain is quite out of the question. The one thing which is necessary is an improvement in methods which shall keep pace with the varying circumstances of subjective and objective existence. Such improvements the world is constantly trying to bring about, and when they are accomplished they pass under the name of progress.

The type of person who has derived most benefit from this growth is the one of an even general development, who has no particular gift in any direction. Both heredity and environment have dealt genially with him, so that every part of him has a proportionally even development. Such a person is as a rule very rare. What one generally sees is a moderate general development with an atrophy and hypertrophy in some particular directions. On exactly the same plan does one find physical endowments distributed. The ordinary man is not evenly developed in all his parts. In one case there is a disproportionate strength and growth of the arms, in another the parts of the back are too small, still another has the hypertrophied thigh muscles that a naturally fine bicyclist might have. Or, a man may have an unusual corrosive gastric secretion and thus be especially able to digest food; his neighbor may have an exceedingly well developed tactile apparatus, so that his sense of touch is more than ordinarily keen. Such cases one meets every day; they excite no surprise, simply because they are common. We likewise know from experience that with proper training all these peculiarities and an indefinite number of others like them may be artificially reproduced. By such methods one may bring about changes in an ordinary person's body which would stamp him, if they occurred spontaneously, as quite remarkable.

In such cases of cultivation, one knows the cause of the uncommon development, one explains the phenomena on fairly well understood biological laws, stating that an unusually active metabolism has made unusual nutritional changes necessary, that the tissue involved has, as the result of these changes, thrived and grown beyond what would ordinarily have been its limit, that the particular cells in question have received so much nourishment that their function has broadened proportionally. This principle of development has the widest influence on the body, which often enough produces results that affect the mind.

Thus a condition which temporarily or permanently so controls the blood supply to a part that the balance of its metabolism is disturbed would necessarily dispose the organ in question to heightened or lowered function, according to the direction of disturbance. As an example, one might quote the group of cases of Whitwell, in which "mental and nervous lethargy and torpor," and "no sign of originating mental power," were leading features. He goes on to demonstrate that the condition is due to a "deficient development of the vascular system." He believes that the imperfect growth rests upon too small a heart, aorta, or basal cerebral vessels, so that the cerebral tissues are more or less starved. Where the condition is a permanent one, the mental state is continously dull. Where it is spasmodic, there would be varying phases of mental dulness and lucidity. He traces a direct connection between the virility of the mental powers and the nourishing circulation which in part helps to make an active nutrition possible.

Where an analogous process of hypertrophy takes place in a part or a number of parts, a condition of overgrowth results which may go so far as to disturb every law of conservation of energy. Such a state one calls elephantiasis. The exact causes of it we do not know, but of its general disposition there is sufficient knowledge to allow a man of Ranke's carefulness to attribute it to "perturbations of development during fœtal life." While this statement has the inexactness of generalization, nevertheless it shows in what direction modern thought is tending. It shows us that the scientific world has advanced to the stage where it recognizes that there is much in every human being which, from the time of conception, is susceptible of modification. So long as this is so, the main problem which presents itself lies in the way of using the possibilities of nutrition so as to obtain the best all-around growth.

Where, as in the instance quoted above, there is a one-sided development, the full potentialities of the individual are not conserved. It is plain enough that a man, every part of whose body is well developed, is a better result of training than one whose arms are comparatively over-developed, and whose legs are comparatively under-developed. A man whose senses are fairly keen in all directions is of more use to himself and the community than one who possesses abnormally keen sight and abnormally dull taste or touch or hearing. The harmonious relations of parts are not broken with impunity. The penalty is an ever-increasing unevenness, which is bound to limit the man's usefulness to the narrowest possible limits, to make him more nearly like a machine. Or the process may end in producing curiosities, "freaks," beings whose simple ability does not atone for many-sided uselessness. It is bad enough when this lameness is confined to physical gifts, especially those of a low order. The higher one ascends in the scale of efficiency, the more deplorable are the results.

No matter how undesirable these effects may be in the man, they are infinitely worse in the child, whose growth is in a plastic state of change, who needs all possible nourishment for every part of the economy, who, in the presence of a drifting-off of such nourishment from any part, would suffer not merely from a partial vitality, but rather an obliteration of the functions involved. A condition like this is unfortunate enough when occurring in the purely physical powers, but when it appears in the higher gifts of the intellect, the emotions, and the character, the person should receive much more sympathy, or even commiseration. He might rightfully regard himself as the victim of hard circumstances, which have placed him in a position somewhat like that of a cripple.

It is easy to see the close analogy underlying both physical and mental gifts. The same classification fits equally well to both, the same nutritional laws act as surely in the case of one as in that of the other. The same laws of cell-growth, cell-hypertrophy and cell-atrophy are common. One naturally makes the same distinctions between feeble mental power as a whole, uneven mental power, and strong general development. The first class one calls the feeble-minded or defective, the second is what one meets in the ordinary man and woman, and the third constitutes the highly gifted. Between these there are many gradations whose nomenclature varies with individual views.

One of the commonest phenomena is to find a person who congenitally or artificially has a leaning in one direction, which he develops as far as he can. Such a person is called "talented," or, in cases of marked development, he is named a "genius." At the same time, there is the greatest confusion in the interpretation of this word "genius." Some people take it to mean unusual intellectual brightness in general, some thus designate an unusual relation of associational ideas, some call by this name an hypertrophied function in any branch of intellectual effort. But in the last analysis most people apply the term to a man who has achieved great distinction in any of the arts, mostly those of literature, painting, sculpture and music. As a rule, there is so little of common agreement on the subject that he who is a genius to one person is not such to the next one. The definition of the quality of genius is as multiform as the number of definers increases. One person calls it "the power of continuity," another "the faculty of application," another "the possibility of original composition," another "the power of leading one's time in any department of intellectual effort." Some persons wish to extend the appellation, speaking of a "moral genius" or a "philanthropic genius" or a "political genius." I have even seen the phrase "pugilistic genius." And doubtless this last holds as good a title to soundness of doctrine as many of the others. The main idea seems to be to include in this class any man who shows a marked gift in any direction. Under this rule the idiot, Blind Tom, must likewise be termed a genius; a "mind-reader" like the late Washington Bishop is surely entitled to be called a genius; a convict who, by infinite patience and an unlimited supply of time, makes a toy log house out of thousands of minute pieces of wood is also a genius; a man with a deep knowledge of human weaknesses and necessities, who, by trickery, bribery and corruption, plays one faction against another, until he holds the political course of a municipality in the hollow palm of his hand, is likewise a genius. Anybody and everybody, from the highest to the lowest, who makes an impress upon the minds of men, is just as clearly entitled, according to the diverse and conflicting opinions generally held, to this glorious name as the greatest soul that ever shed a freshening ray of light into the hearts and souls of us common mortals.

The true genius is the grand, the awe-inspiring, the soul-compelling figure in human ideals. He is supposed to stand and should stand on a lofty eminence, bathed in clouds, giving out a gorgeous radiance that clears the tangled paths of petty mankind who thus may run their course to the peaceful resting-place of a quiet and forgotten grave. The god-like impulse in him should carry his thoughts and acts beyond the reach of frail temptation into the serene land of noble creative accomplishment. His life should be the summation of men's hopes, their longings, their aspirations. The consistent course of such a being's career should be the beacon light to which future generations might fix their eyes, as the helmsman in a wide sea turns his gaze towards the Northern Star. Not a spot should sully the pure lustre of his reputation, not a blemish should disfigure the entirety of his praise. As a consistent whole, his life and works should stand in priceless grandeur, so that no man could raise against them a carping tone. But, alas! one does not see such careers. On the contrary, one sees lives that are pieced and patched, lives that may have a strong melody running through them, but marred and cheapened by discords and over-tones. For each great gift one finds a corresponding weakness, near each line of brightness one sees a spot of black. The idol's head may be of gold, but his body and feet are apt to be made of baser metals and clay.

The more closely one thinks about the matter, the more clearly one sees that what we mean by *the genius* is an ideal, pure and simple. Short of this one can find no line which will accurately mark off the so-called genius from the talented man, any more than one can differentiate the talented from the ordinary man. What one does find is a varying development in this direction or in that, a greater vitality in one line or another; in other words, a greater production of energy in some group or groups of cells, which have had the advantage of a proportionately great nourishment. The world would understand the matter much better, would be able better to appreciate the lesson of superlative accomplishment, if it would speak of a great man as a gifted man, rather than a genius. It would understand that great gifts do not come arbitrarily and without reason; it knows from common experience that the more favorable the training and environment of any part of the body are, the better will its functions be. Further, it would know that naturally great gifts, like smaller ones, may be developed and improved. The way to an indefinitely extended betterment would thus become plainer, and the efforts to secure this betterment would then surely, even if slowly, follow.

The lesson of greatness is not complete unless it is studied along with its accompanying weaknesses. A great man is unjustly dealt with when only one part of him is known. And unquestionably, the community is most fairly treated by receiving the most faithful impressions. An estimate of Cæsar, which shows nothing but his remarkable administrative capacity, removes him so far from ordinary methods of judgment that what one sees is not the presentment of the man, but rather a projection of one phase of him. A much more realistic and helpful view would include the weaknesses that were sufficient to keep him far from the pedestal of the demi-god. The bloody Napoleon, great in the conquest of armies, in the making of countless widows and orphans, in dismembering states, has his limitations so strongly marked, that if time could wipe out the trail of destructive ambition which he left behind him, the best part of his deeds would be destroyed. The hypertrophy of a single faculty was strongly marked in him. Among men of military fame Washington, in the full and rounded development of the whole range of man, was infinitely his superior, infinitely more worthy of admiration. Of the two, the former played the part of ruthless and selfish destroyer; he is one of the great personages of the world who is least deserving of respect for his characteristic ability. Among other deficiencies, his lack of moral sense — a constituent element in the cerebral equation — was starved, was shriveled. The American, on the other hand, approached much nearer to the ideal of development in every part. While not by any means perfect, nevertheless his great gifts showed so large and bountiful a range, that the world may point to him with highest pride as an earnest of what manhood may possibly come to be.

Take a man of quite different parts for an example

—Wagner. The range of his gifts was wide enough to embrace the domains of music, literature and stage management, which is indeed a wide field. In these arts his hand was that of a master, and all the world is now swinging censers before his shrine. While appreciating his gifts, one ought likewise to recognize how unworthy of admiration he was in many other respects; one ought clearly to see that he embodied a one-sided growth, a partial nutrition. Doubtless one might, with truth, say that the one-sidedness of this nutrition showed itself in the eccentricities and want of sanity which unquestionably characterized part of his work. The pathological intensity of "Tristan and Isolde," and the esoteric mysticism in "Die Götterdämmerung," are far from being the product of a normal and admirable cerebral balance. Placed next to the joyous healthfulness of "Die Meistersinger," they must forever represent high intellectual action, plus unusual cortical irritation such as one would not expect to find in the healthy and even results of a desirable nutrition.

The more closely one examines the great men of the world, the more is one convinced of the satisfactory nature of the classification here advocated. At the same time, there is not the least desire to subtract one jot or tittle from their fame and its reward. On the contrary, there is the greatest reason, because these gifted men were not the perfectly developed creatures that unwise partisans construe them to be, to laud their great deeds that were done in spite of collateral imperfections. The fact remains the same, that the true genius, the man of noble and complete development, has never, so far as is known, existed. Doubtless the one who comes nearest the mark is Goethe. In him there occurred a wonderful combination of the artistic and scientific faculties, the like of which has never existed in any other man. His breadth of range was wonderful, the catholicity of his sympathies, the scope of his imagination, immense. His personality was deeply impressive, his cultural influence was very great. But even he was not evenly rounded. Even he suffered from a partial development which showed an imperfect functional activity in at least one direction. His moral acts were distinctly within the range of adverse criticism, and for them there can be no other just opinion than a lack of proper development. The world must surely come to recognize that a perfect exercise of every part of psychical action is the most desirable thing within the bounds of human endeavor. This would constitute the nearest approach to the perfect man of which we are able to conceive. On this principle, moral development is fully as important as that which includes proficiency in literature, scientific, or artistic departments. No matter how far one may consider ethics to be composed of emotional or intellectual elements, the same general rule would govern it. So long as one knows that cerebral molecular action is the origin of the energy which elaborates thought and nervous impulse, one must surely conclude that the ideal development, the development which represents the highest point of efficiency for the individual, as well as the community, is the one that will invigorate every nerve cell in all its ramification. Not only is this the goal for which the world must strive, but also it is the standard by which every human being should be measured. The contemplation of the ideal is the one method by which the acts and action of human beings are improved. Nothing less can be enough of an incentive nor hold enough of rigid exactness by which the growth of succeeding times may be guided.

This rule, when applied to the precocious child, — the child-genius, — is of overweening importance. Such a child necessarily attracts great attention, receives unmeasured praise even for faulty performance. His unusual faculty is unusual from the standpoint of childhood, a time which one associates with so incomplete a development that its work one expects to be petty, disconnected, without the concentration and finish that mature strength of tissue alone can confer. By respecting the unstable weakness of immaturity, we know that the person thereby receives opportunity to feed the delicate nerve substance, to build up a machine that will count efficient deeds as the normal expression of its function rather than a drain upon its very substance. The difference between exacting a certain high standard in work from an adult, and attempts to extort the same efforts from a child, is the difference between drawing from a capital sum or the interest which that sum normally yields. In the one case the original faculty is undisturbed, in the other it is decreased or obliterated. However, this is not the only or the worst result; for the work of precocious children is not as a rule of very much benefit outside of the gratification of curiosity. Beyond this one fact, there is hardly any reason for allowing such children to show their abilities. Moreover, there is hardly a single branch of human industry that they have in any way improved.

In addition, and as something much more serious, is the unevenness, the one-sided growth of mind and character that must of necessity come about. Where a normal supply of energy is being drafted into the service of a certain comparatively small area of cerebral tissue, the remaining portions must necessarily receive a smaller amount of nourishment. The person's whole habit of mind undergoes a change. His mental processes work within a small circle, and progress beyond that circle may be gained only with the greatest difficulty. He realizes facts and thoughts very much as a child sees various colors through a tinted glass; the real colors are thereby changed so far from their true shade as not to be recognizable.

In physics one knows that a luminous ray in passing from one body to another undergoes a bending, a reflection. The angle at which one is unable to perceive the ray is called the critical angle. This angle of total reflection varies with different substances, being in some exceedingly small. In similar ways one may fitly say that in the mind of the man who in childhood was precocious, there is apt to be an angle of total reflection that is unusually narrow. He has suffered a series of changes which makes a broad development and a consequently broad life out of the question. By the very act of precocious consumption of nerve energy, normal metabolism must give way to unusual tissue changes, with abnormal symptoms in mind and character.

In these times, one hears much talk about mental and moral degeneracy. The term is loosely used, and is meant to designate all sorts of people who show unfavorable psychical characteristics, especially in the ways of moral weakness, intellectual superficiality, lack of concentrated effort, a craving for the outlandish, the *bizarre*, even the shocking, elements in life. Inordinate conceit is supposed to be one of its symptoms, especially where there is no good ground for unusual self-praise. Recalcitration to discipline, repugnance to the settled and rigid conditions of life, are commonly encountered. Irreverence for rightful authority and the creation of new gods are supposed to be commonly seen. In other words, a perturbation of the nervous system exists which does not permit of a natural expression of vitality. The theory is held that the strain and stress of modern life, with its whirl and rush, its astounding upheavals of settled ideas which gigantic improvements have introduced, its irreverence, its impatience, its thirst for luxury, have brought this condition of things into existence. Whether or not this is the cause, whether or not these characteristics flourish in greater abundance now then formerly, at all events, traits like them are merely evidences of poor development, of poorly nourished cerebral cells, of distorted streams of energy that are following the ragged lines of least resistance.

This is exactly the result that one would expect from cerebral precocity; it is the outcome of disturbed relations which can be known only by the disturbance in their classic functions. Degeneracy is not a disease, it is merely a symptom, the cause of which is a defiance of ordinary laws which dominate the lowest as well as the highest of men. It may be exterminated, but only by a plan of life which looks out for primal conditions rather than remedial measures. As soon as the child's main business in life is seen to consist in proper eating and proper assimilation of food, in proper sleep, in proper recreation and exercise, in proper instruction, in the right and healthy exercise of his emotions, as well as his intellect and body, the symptom must disappear. The child should no more be allowed to assume great burdens involving mental strain and excitement than he should be permitted to play with dynamite. The difference in the ultimate outcome is partly one of time. But one main fact holds good: great deeds require corresponding exertion. Where the economy, by its maturity and nice development, has acquired full power, such exertion is merely normal and healthful exercise. When it is immature, unstable, unripe, such efforts exhaust its vitality, distort its regular outlines, undermine its creative possibilities. The problem is not a hard one; it requires nothing more than plain and clear and sane thought.

CHAPTER X

INSTITUTIONAL LIFE IN THE DEVELOPMENT OF THE CHILD

THE care of children in institutions — what one might call the substitute care of children — comes next in importance to the care of them at home. In fact, it is only by comparing it to home training that one can judge of the worth of the discipline which an institution gives. Moreover, the ideal that should constantly be kept in mind is that of furnishing methods which will most surely bring about the results that home life of a high order is able to do. This has almost always seemed impossible; the general respect for parental influence and authority has been so great that no adequate substitute for it has been considered possible. "Any home is better than a Home" has been the cry; and even in cases of marked deficiency of favorable environment, the opinion is stoutly advocated that the interests of the State and the individuals concerned are best preserved by keeping, no matter what the circumstances, the family circle intact. Formerly this was held in so extreme a degree that failure on the part of parents to provide properly for their children's physical and moral growth was not considered sufficient reason for breaking family ties. Flagrant instances of neglect, of cruelty, of viciousness, were regarded with complacency. The child was the father's chattel, existing under absolute rights of possession. And in recent times when the movement to establish children's aid societies began to assume a definite form, much difficulty was experienced in overcoming the feeling that the rights of parents were paramount. Therefore, where investigation revealed full evidence of immorality or almost fatal abuse, the cry still went up that "any home is better than a Home!"

Now, however, things have changed somewhat. People recognize that the family is of the highest use to the State when children are so reared that their mental and physical faculties receive sufficient opportunity to expand in a fairly decent fashion. They have come to see that parental authority is not necessarily wisely administered, but on the contrary may give unlimited opportunity for wrong-doing, that parental example may, instead of leading children in the ways of peace and health, drag them down to the lowest depths of misery and viciousness. Under such circumstances the "home" becomes a plague-spot. Even under milder circumstances, but where rugged virtues do not flourish, the home may be so far from providing a normal nutrition for body and mind that its value is doubtful. The need for a substitute then becomes imperative, and the whole question resolves itself into an inquiry about the best methods of accomplishing the desired ends.

In looking over the matter, the observer notices a curious fact: that the oldest and most civilized communities are not necessarily the ones that have made most progress. Rather, they are the most conservative, where the belief in old-time rights is most firmly held, or where the feeling for non-interference is strongest. In such communities one is most apt to find great institutions for the care of orphaned and abused children, which are architecturally fine, richly endowed, which are sedulously visited by the charitably inclined. Nevertheless, in spite of these advantages, their wards commonly do not turn out well; as a rule, they do not grow into men and women of the highest type. In fact, this is what people expect, and all manner of consideration for shortcomings in a person is made who has had the misfortune to grow up as an asylum child. The cry again is heard: "Any home is better than a Home!"

In dealing with institutions of this kind, one comes across certain phenomena which occur regularly in almost all cases. One finds large masses of children marked off from the rest of the community, commonly wearing a special uniform which emphasizes their segregation, controlled in the large majority of instances by a man or woman whose main excellence is a faculty of administrative discipline, which brings about an appearance of outward neatness and a show of meek submission on the part of the charges of the institution to the visiting board; one finds a hard and fast routine which being designed for the management of all is generally fitted for no one individual; one finds that often useless and trivial occupations are taught, which tend to increase the institutional revenues and make a brave show of employing a large number of "hands"; one finds that the children are brought up in huge buildings where the ordinary duties of life are arranged on a wholesale plan, where the actual conditions of everyday existence are unknown, where the true value of individual independence, of money, of personal self-respect, of personal affection, are barely suggested. And where the State pays a *per capita* share of the expenses, one finds a disposition to get as many children into one institution as is possible; for in reckoning the support of large numbers, the individual cost is in inverse ratio to the number supported. As a result of all this, the ends to be expected in an advantageous development are not by any means kept in sight.

One must keep in mind that the care of these children involves a different method of treatment than that of the ordinary child in the ordinary home. Many of them having come from an impoverished stock have a predisposition to weakness in mind and body, still more have lived their short lives in surroundings characterized by want or ignorance or stupidity or viciousness. Many of them bear the hall-mark of their most unfortunate environment. They are correspondingly ready to fall into developmental distortions and are correspondingly hard to be kept within the lines of a straight growth. Far more than the ordinary child should they be watched and nurtured, — not only for their own sakes, but also for that of the community of which they form an important part. When one comes to think that in the State of New York, one out of every two hundred and fifty-one of the population is supported from the public funds, the necessity immediately becomes apparent of properly caring for these wards of the State, to the end of converting them from incumbrances into useful, valuable citizens. The mere fact that they have no natural guardians makes the necessity of caring for them lie all the more heavily on the community which is ultimately affected by their successful or unsuccessful development.

Keeping these things in mind, one can say very little for the methods now used in this State. Although we know that children follow their enveloping influences very closely, and that therefore their daily companions are important factors in determining what they are to be, nevertheless, the system in question puts dozens of children of the same age together, on much the same plan as similar kinds of merchandise are assorted. Naturally, there are no higher examples to be followed, and children do not progress so rapidly as under better auspices they would. Even in infancy one can plainly notice this fact. These little creatures look, act, and really are far otherwise than the ordinary baby in good surroundings. Their want of mental as well as physical activity is so plainly apparent as to be visible even to non-professional observers. From such a source comes the remark that "institution babies are tolerably lethargic." They are lethargic because their vitality has been sapped away, and one might with equal truth say that institution babies are tolerably withered. Even more striking is a fact that can be vouched for by any physician who has had much experience in hospital wards for babies. Such patients languish in institutions although their food and care are fairly good. In fact, the same food and care, if provided with the surroundings of a home, will often bring the little one to blooming health and vigor. The reason is not hard to find out. The gist of the matter is, that the care of a baby is not meant to be arranged on a wholesale plan. He needs personal attention, and without it his body withers. An even greater effect has a too strongly marked routine upon his mind. The routine means machine-like repetition, day after day and week after week, of the same or similar acts. It is the opposite of the change, the varying activity and the spontaneity of individual training. An adult whose growth is finished, whose organism is at rest, might possibly exist without much injury in a condition of stagnation. His needs lie mainly in the way of repair of used-up tissue. But with the growing infant or child, the demands are far greater. They look for the elaboration of entirely new material upon which functional development rests. And where such healthful exercise is deficient, the expected development cannot appear. Naturally, then, one finds that children massed in large institutions are backward, are prone to stupidity, are lacking in a healthy mental curiosity. Their spontaneity is crushed by rules and regulations that are not framed with a clear view to their best interests.

In order to subserve those interests, the person in charge of the institution should be of remarkable strength of mind and character. By slow degrees people are beginning to appreciate the necessity of employing as teachers such persons as have proved themselves thoroughly capable. The opinion is slowly — but very slowly — gaining ground, that the real teacher is not some young woman in need of pin money, or a girl who wishes to keep herself busy in the time between graduation and marriage. The part of the public that pretends to think is steadily coming to feel that those who have control of numbers of children for an important part of each working day, should be carefully selected for this great responsibility by both training and natural fitness. The more charitably minded may hold that parents by the very fact of parenthood come to possess a special faculty for the training and care of their offspring. But with the teacher, who cannot pretend to have any reason for such a faculty, quite a different idea must be in force. With her, the matter is and should be merely that of a business, a vocation, at the most, a well-loved vocation. Therefore, she should have every possible advantage which may enable her to prosecute her duties in the best possible manner. If this is true of the ordinary teacher, a similar train of thought will more imperatively apply to the superintendent of an institution for children. But it is with the greatest rarity that one finds the position conferred on any such principle of choice. The ordinary incumbent is a man who has had political training and political influence, or a superior sort of workman who has shown some manner of practical ability, or a relative of a person in authority in the management. Among some of the superintendents of whom I know, there are retired or unsuccessful business men, a retired insurance agent, a carpenter, a former watchman, an assistant matron in a hospital, two former teachers and two clergymen. While it is possible that all of these persons may be active and zealous to do what is right,—as far as they can see the right,—nevertheless, I seriously doubt that they have a respectable share of the special training and knowledge which are absolutely necessary to the realization of the possibilities of their positions.

As far as one can judge, their common feeling is one of full satisfaction when their institutions have no violent outbreaks of epidemic diseases, when the children have a clean exterior, when they show the effects of wholesome drilling so that all of them can make the same sort of obeisance, can march meekly and in regular order, can answer certain lists of questions without too much confusion. Most of these superintendents, I believe, feel that the children are very fortunate in having so much care, so many advantages, and that the fact of their being dependent upon charity should make them supremely thankful for any fate that is better than starvation. As a matter of fact, such a system is as unprofitable as one could possibly imagine. Society has the keenest interests in the outcome of these many lives, which have the prospect of inefficiency and pauperism before them. For each has the same range of possibilities as more fortunate children, each one has the same liability to being crushed. In the hands of a very wise guardian they might have unlimited potentialities for good, and with a better system these wards of the State might come to be parts of its strongest bulwarks. The natural conclusion is, that the welfare of so many lives requires the highest skill for its care. The superintendent of an institution for children should represent the highest type of guardian that the community can afford, a person who is able by training, experience and ability to have broad views, wise policies and a sympathetic discernment of character that will prevent his looking at his charges as so many little animals that are to be kept in subjection.

Of course, one might say that no human wisdom is great enough to govern the development of every individual child in a large institution. That may be true; but it is not more true than that a superior man can accomplish more than an inferior. It is hard to mark off the limits of what the properly selected person can do. But besides this one factor, there are other considerations to be taken into account. A child who is brought up in huge dormitories and dining-rooms, in marble-paved, steam-heated halls, who sees the world through the bars of a fence, who is inspected with the same curiosity as the animals in the Zoo, who goes to bed with no more caressing sound than the clang of a retiring bell, who receives no more affection than the share that a stranger can distribute among dozens or hundreds, who lives and moves as part of a great machine, has little chance of developing in a way that will call into life all the range of activities of which his organization is susceptible. Therefore, it has been said, truly enough, that such children are lethargic, show "a want of pluck, dependence on others, inability to shift for themselves, characteristics which develop into the grown pauper." When such children are old enough to be put out in the world, their chances of survival must be pitiably small; they must be thoroughly unprepared to fight the battles that await every man and woman; they may be considered analogous to immigrants from another world. To expect from them the same grasp of affairs, the same self-restraint, the same tenacity of purpose, and the same moderation in conduct that we look for in ordinary, more fortunate citizens, is not quite logical. Thus they are forced into a class by themselves; although the world will not allow them to transgress its rules, nevertheless, it does not furnish a special code that is better adapted to their peculiar condition.

As things now are, there is no personal responsibility for the children in large institutions. Those in control are sedulously guarding the *institution* rather than the individual children for whom the institution exists. Most of these institutions are controlled by private persons who have absolute authority in their management. This might be good enough, if such persons were generally in possession of the most desirable qualifications for the positions. But, as a rule, they are men who have been selected on account of money donations or similar reasons. The consequent result is that these kind and charitable persons feel most interest in the business affairs of the institution; they believe that these affairs are the main objects of care;

partly, perhaps, because such are the things which they best understand. In the meanwhile, there is no one to look after the individual child, who is no more thought of than is a single lamb in a large flock. As yet, there is hardly enough interest felt in this important part of the population to call forth a general and constant inquiry into methods of management. Occasionally, some one utters a protest, such as Mrs. Josephine Shaw Lowell did in the report of the New York Board of Charities for 1890. There she said: "New York City supports an average population of about 14,000 boys and girls, at an expense of $1,500,000 annually, in institutions controlled by private individuals. . . . There is no official of New York City who knows or has a right to know whether these children are trained in idleness or industry, in virtue or vice."

Even if one rejects so harsh a possibility as being trained in vice, one has still a multitude of conditions that may be almost as bad. Among them one is bound to find deceit, a want of open frankness, a lack of principle, a disposition to cringe and fawn, that are destructive to a healthy mental tone. Most of all are these acquired characteristics not distinctive of the state of mind which produces fine men and women. From the start, such children are condemned to the likelihood of weak and petty characters, which the experiences of mature life are not likely to strengthen.

As far as the question of industrial training in large

institutions goes, very little that is pleasant can be said. In most cases, the occupations are those involving but little skill, they are generally of a low grade, and do little to train either mind or body. The children are kept at a method of employment that rarely varies, that blunts and stupefies nascent energy by violations of almost all the rules of healthful development. Steady work in such ways as picking hair, making paper bags and the many similarly trivial things which one here finds, may, especially when well paid for by the charitably inclined, add considerable amounts to the revenues of the institution. But this is gained at the expense of brain and nerve energy in the child. But even where the nature of the work is more profitable, one may still be sure that the children cannot gain thereby. For the essential characteristic of the child body and mind is the inability to concentrate attention or efforts excepting in a small degree and for a short time. Thus, no steady employment, even where it does not make a slave of the child, can do anything but harm. To obtain a proper diversity of employment is practically impossible in a great asylum, even where the ruling powers would be willing to follow any plan that could improve the results of their work. One should keep in mind that children, whose permanent welfare is a matter of importance, should never be expected to do work for the sake of an immediate money return. For such work requires too much concentration of effort and attention to be undertaken with safety. Even under the luxurious surroundings of a modern asylum, such work has a number of features in common with "child-slavery."

Too much stress cannot be laid upon the isolating circumstances of institutional life. Nothing is easier or more certain in results than to crush and cow a child by marking him off with unfortunate circumstances from the common life of young children. Even in so mild a case as some slight physical deformity, where the child's attention is thrown in upon himself, he straightway begins to feel himself apart from the rest of the world, he shrinks together like a withered flower. He loses confidence in himself, feels that he is in an unfavorable and subordinate position; he comes to believe that the world is a harsh and bitter place for him and such as he. In the case of an "institution child," such effects are many times magnified. His home, his dress, the demeanor and discipline of everyday life, all impress him with the belief that fate has dealt differently and more harshly with him than with other people whom he sees. He realizes that his position is one of subjection, and of necessity he must crouch down to the level of a conquered soul. In such an environment, it would require a remarkable child to give a good account of himself, especially from the standpoint of final development. Even the one detail of a common uniform is sufficient in itself to shut out the light from a child's mind and soul, and turn him into a creature who really needs one's pity. But when his little existence is filled with such details, when his environment keeps constantly in his mind the facts of his unfortunate and contemptible position, he becomes a victim of a system which chokes and starves while it pretends to nourish. It is, in truth, a sort of slavery, but slavery that is so tricked out and bedizened as to pass for a joyous philanthropy. One of the results of the whole unfortunate problem is that the community, while thinking to rescue its children — an integral part of itself — from a miserable and unprofitable life, is really doing a great deal in the way of making such a life inevitable.

However, a better method than this time-honored one is easy to find. Knowing as much as we do about the necessities of a child's development, being certain that child-life flourishes best in a natural home, we must find the solution of caring for the State's wards by providing surroundings that will closely imitate those of the home. Unquestionably, this is possible, and, to a certain extent, it has been done in various places. The noteworthy success which Herr Wichern's Rauhe Haus at Hamburg achieved, duplicated to a certain extent at the Metteay institution at Tour, showed clearly enough the path that progress is to take. Here a real attempt was made to form a home. Instead of great and cumbersome institutions, the plan of forming small colonies was begun, which reminds one strongly of the schools which Pestalozzi and Froebel formed. The plan was devised for the "substitution of individual care for mechanical manipulation of masses and the development of energy, nature, wit, and common sense that follow from the separation into small groups with whom the teacher or nurse comes into personal contact." So good an example was bound to be tried elsewhere. To be sure, in many cases the efforts were tentative, but, nevertheless, they showed progress, and obtained better results than under the older system. But if one had no other or more modern models than those of Pestalozzi's and Froebel's schools, most of all before a general acquaintance with their wise methods and fine results brought too many scholars, one would be close upon the right manner of caring for orphaned and abused children. The motto that was ever before the minds of these two lovable and loving men was: "Come, let us live with our children." They really shared their lives with their charges, — studied with them, worked with them in all manner of ordinary ways, played with them, ate and slept with them. Between teacher and scholar, or one might better say guardian and ward, there existed the common bonds of mutual love, mutual welfare, mutual interests. These children, instead of having a parent's oversight for a small part of the day and the cold comfort of a stranger's attention for the greater part, associated constantly with a foster-father who was much wiser, more thoughtful, than most decent parents are. There were a constant play and exercise of mind and body. And not until the system by its own growth grew unwieldy, and thus lost its proper characteristics, did it cease to serve as one of the best methods of rearing children with which we are acquainted.

Coming back to present times and instances, let us cite the cases of Victoria and New South Wales. These colonies, in an attempt to improve their ways, sought to abolish institutions by a system of boarding out their orphan children. This method, while too provisional and not sufficiently homogeneous, had some advantages in doing away with the crowding of children together in large numbers. Outside of everything else, they gained at least a recognition of the important fact that children may not with safety be herded together in large numbers. The value of this idea began to be felt even beyond these colonies, — even in conservative Europe, — and gradually concessions were made to it. These concessions came slowly, as one would expect; for old communities with difficulty change their ways. But even more thoroughly did it make an impress in the

United States. Massachusetts, in particular, tried to better itself, and was the first to institute a State system of preventive work by boarding out its orphans and deserted children. Some good results were almost immediately apparent. In the important detail of infant mortality, a startling change occurred. In the first year of the new system, the percentage of deaths fell from ninety-seven per cent to fifty per cent. In the following year, it declined to thirty per cent, and after that varied from ten to twenty per cent.

Still another effect was promptly felt. Where the old-time system was in vogue, with its large institutions which indiscriminately received undeserving as well as deserving cases, children were too easily entrusted to its care. Proximity to the children and ease in communicating with them, as well as the seeming ease of reclaiming them whenever the parents pleased, made commitments to the asylum very frequent, much more frequent than was necessary. But where the large institutions were abolished and the children were scattered over a large territory, the feeling of parental care sprang up again, with the natural result that offspring were not so lightly abandoned. Thus in New York State, under our antiquated system, the community supports one in every two hundred and fifty-one of the population; but in Massachusetts, with a wiser method, the ratio was reduced to one in nine hundred and ninety-five. And in Michigan, under a still more rigorous rule, only one in ten thousand required support. To clinch the argument on the other side, one might cite the case of New Hampshire, which recently decided to support dependent children in private institutions at the public expense, with the same freedom from restrictions as one sees in New York and California. As one would expect, the regular results of increased dependence began to assert themselves. In addition, it is in place to quote the success of the Lyman School and the State Industrial School at Lancaster, both carried on under the methods in use in Massachusetts, where the success has been noteworthy. They have proved how possible it is to reduce the evils from which society has so long suffered, to convert worthless material into approximately valuable material, to make a large proportion of the deserted, the abused, the practically brutalized population into decent citizens. Such a change is a truly remarkable one, and has a bearing upon the future welfare and improvement of society that cannot be too highly appreciated.

Keeping these instances in mind, and combining them with the more theoretical truths of a child's development which we know, the way in which the wards of the State should be brought up is fairly clear. All thought of massing them in large institutions, whether conducted under private or public management, should be absolutely put aside. The more one appreciates how feeble in stable conditions and how strong in potential changes an infant is, the more clearly one sees that he should have more than food and clothing. The additional element may be supplied by individual care and the willingness to undergo self-sacrifice which comes from personal attachment. Such care and attachment the normal woman, fairly well brought up, is capable and willing to give. One of the main needs is to entrust the children to as good a representative of normal womanhood as it is possible to find. That it is easily possible to realize the opportunity to enlist a high class of women in this work is clearly proved by the readiness with which such women agree to adopt young children, to take upon themselves the whole responsibility of their physical and mental care. Mrs. Richardson, of the Massachusetts State Board of Lunacy and Charity, gives evidence on this point, when she says that "in recent years the opportunities for obtaining homes by legal adoption into good families have been so great that it is rarely that a child reaches the age of three years without being permanently and satisfactorily provided for." One might confidently say that these opportunities would be still more plentiful if women were convinced — as they doubtless will be — of the safety of adopting an infant of unknown parentage. When the community come to realize that a child's environment is as a rule more important than his heredity, there will be still less necessity for great infant asylums. In fact, the only institution of this kind that is permissible is a receiving station, a sort of clearing house, which shall be used as headquarters where the routine business of placing children and overseeing them is carried on.

Such children as are not adopted should be put in homes of not more than ten little ones. These homes could be grouped in colonies so that the proper authorities could easily oversee them. Supplies could be purchased in large quantities and delivered on requisition according to need. Each home could be immediately controlled by a cottage "mother," who should have a natural and full authority. The children should be kept in this manner until they were able by apprenticeship or individual work to support themselves. The close association of years would form the strongest bonds between the foster-mother and her charges, and the small number of children entrusted to each woman would make possible the growth of affection, individual interest, and the feeling of responsibility. Each child, as he grew up, would go through the ordinary useful experience of the ordinary home, the only experience which is able to fit him for the duties of worker, spouse and parent. Here would be a feeling of solidarity, a sense of active and passive ownership, a happy conviction of having a place in the world. The education of the children could be conducted in village schools in the same way that public education is generally administered. And the children would finally come to take their places in the world with connections and memories that would be as binding, as well known, and as respectable as those of people with a natural and honorable parentage.

The main object of these cottage homes would be to counterfeit, as closely as possible, the real home as we know it, in its healthy phases. The same methods of control, of occupation, of clothing, of food, of recreation, could be employed in one as well as in the other. The conditions of actual, practical life would be equally illustrated in both. The number of children in each home would be so restricted that each child would receive a fairly proper amount of attention. As a result, his character and individuality would have an opportunity to assert themselves. At the same time, the very important factor of the finer feelings would not be neglected. For the number of children living together would be small enough to encourage the closest interdependencies between them and the cottage mother. One could look forward to the future of these children with the same confidence with which one regards the outlook of well-cared-for children in ordinary life.

Another fact of importance is that such work would appeal to many women of decided abilities who are either idle or engaged in less valuable work. For the same reasons that the professional nursing of the sick is now so eagerly taken up by a high class of women, this calling would be popular. But in addition, there are many additional reasons, based upon the opportunity for exercising affection, for forming much more permanent ties, for having a very definite influence in the world, why an even higher grade of women would gladly assume this calling as a life work. Most of all, if the applicants for positions as foster-mothers received an equally valuable training as trained nurses enjoy, the results of their work might gratify very high expectations.

That children brought up under substitute care can have a successful training has been proved by the course pursued at Girard College. Although this institution has the disadvantage of great size, as well as the fact that its charges are not accepted in infancy, thus depriving them of the good effects of careful and systematic oversight in their earliest years, nevertheless, the general methods of government are so superior to what one usually finds in institutions for orphans, that the results are, after all, not surprising. Children may not be accepted in infancy, but, on the other hand, their residence in the institution may continue until they are of eighteen years of age. Their guardians and instructors are of a high class, and on account of their permanent and responsible positions, as well as their mental superiority, come to have a real interest in the boys, that shows itself in the existence of affectionate relationship between pupil and teacher. The inmates, instead of feeling that they are outcasts and pariahs, have a true pride in their surroundings, and act it out in their later lives. For such reasons as these, President Fetteroff is able to say: "Judging from what I see of our graduates, I am inclined to think that they do better in life than the same number of boys picked from the public schools." And this occurs, in spite of the non-natural and artificial environment produced by guardians who take up the work as a profession. It does not need an unusually clear sight to see that if the State's children were from the beginning brought up under still more favorable auspices, if they enjoyed the blessing of individual care, affection and training, if their associations and examples were of the same nature as one finds in good families, if their practical experiences were such as to fit them for the demands of actual life, one would not have to think of institutions for children as the breeding nests of pauperism, vice, and crime. In the community, as it now exists, there is every element which is necessary to the realization of this plan; but instead of being wisely used, it is wasted. Too much money is now spent; too much effort on the part of philanthropic persons of all sorts is scattered over a ragged system; too many lives are spoiled. In the face of all this, so long as the general public is willing to learn and apply some plain biological truths, there is a prospect of an immense betterment. Much of the so-called defective population can be turned into really valuable citizens, who not only would render unnecessary the vast expenses now necessary for charities and corrections, but would also be fertile producers and upholders of what is conservative and fine in the community. The sooner we come to forget the idea that the dependent children of the State are a burden, and come to recognize that they are so much raw material waiting to be developed, the sooner shall we gain the reward of a wise self-interest, of common sense, of broad ideals.

CHAPTER XI

THE PROFESSION OF MATERNITY

THE remarkable progress of the higher education of women is a matter of everyday comment. Notwithstanding the opposition which every comparatively new movement naturally meets, the belief in it has grown in every direction; so that it is common to find families where the young women have had the same training as their brothers, where, moreover, they have shown so good an intellectual receptivity that the higher education of women, as is claimed by its adherents, has thoroughly justified itself. Besides this, so many women have entered professional callings of all kinds, that the old-time claim of difference in intellectual function between them and men has seemingly been forced out of existence. In addition, one meets not only women doctors, women lawyers, architects and preachers, but also those who have entered the non-professional employments. And now it seems that there is no occupation belonging exclusively to men. While this tendency on the face of it is sufficiently remarkable, nevertheless, the change in methods and opinions which underlie it are still more noteworthy.

The reproach of uselessness, frivolity and petty ornamentation has been laid against the education of women even more than against that of their brothers and fathers. For years back the charge was made that the main object of their training was decorative. And there is no doubt that the charge was true. Not only were the methods of instruction exceedingly faulty, but also the subjects of instruction were plainly designed for the effect it might have upon the estimation in which the girls were held. The main consideration sought was to make them *seem* educated, refined, endued with the characteristics of the most favorably placed class in the community. Such a class was supposed to be the rich, the leisure class, people who were beyond the need of useful and productive work, who therefore had the opportunity of placing most stress upon the refinements, the luxuries and the unnecessary things in life. The fact that these persons were able to buy the services of those who did the common, everyday work of the world placed the latter in a seemingly inferior position. Each person, feeling himself somewhat higher in the scale than those in the class below him, and aiming to equal the circumstances and opportunities of the rank above him, strove to obtain the characteristic marks of superiority. These marks were usually evidences of luxury, *luxury-fetiches*, things which argued the possession of more than what was really essential to life or even comfort.

This is one of the main reasons why so many unnecessary elements have been included in a girl's education. For this reason they have been taught a smattering of French, German and Italian; have been taught a trifle about art and music; have been instructed in the petty details of deportment and elocution, of the humanities. Their demonstrations and use of abilities in these directions have rarely had any real, practical value in the conduct of their lives; but, on the contrary, have added sources of complexity, dissatisfaction and inefficiency. Their attempts at piano-playing, at drawing and painting, at an intelligent demonstration of literary and scientific knowledge, were far from being elevating to themselves or others. Outside of being luxury-fetiches, they had no good reason for existence. Most of all has the training of girls been not appropriate to the highest work of which they were capable, of which, moreover, society stood in greatest need. Therefore, with the spread of information and the broadening of ideas, the necessity of giving them a better and more useful training became more and more apparent. When, on account of changing industrial conditions, the competition in life became severer, when a disposition to laxer ideas concerning the sanctity of rank and caste showed itself, when women began to feel the need economically and morally of occupying positions of greater productive value, the tendency to branch out in any and every line of activity grew with a remarkable vigor. One might with safety say, that they have not observed the bounds of moderation; that in searching for new opportunities, they have at times overstepped the limits set by their functional and social position. As a result, the fields of work formerly held exclusively by men have been more and more energetically invaded by women; industrially the barriers which separated the sexes have been assiduously assailed, until there is now no real line at which one may say that a man's work ends and a woman's begins.

Naturally, there has been a lack of moderation in all this; the hand has swung too far around the dial, until its direction is as eccentric as it ever was. The principal consideration is, that in the strain and stress of active life, no regard is held for what industries may be most profitable to the individual woman and the community. The great idea seems to be that she must do *something*, must earn money, must assume a certain share of active responsibility by going out into the world and grappling with its harsh conditions. To the former ideas of luxury-fetichism she has added the idols of theoretic equality, until the resulting worship is, indeed, a remarkable mixture. Such equality has ever been a strange thing. It mixes real with fancied conditions; true with fictitious needs in human nature; true psychological laws with preconceived notions of necessity. It is apt to long for a state of things that could not be profitable to any one. It is blind, and seeks to go its way regardless of limitations and obstacles that wisdom prompts one to take into account. This idea of equality, in its jealous avarice, tries to obtain a privilege or a right not because it is in itself desirable, but, rather, because one class of people and not another possesses it. The question of the value of such a privilege seems not to be worthy of consideration. Thus, in the matter of the so-called higher education, the demand for a woman's learning Greek, for example, is usually made not because the study of that language is thought to bring with it any considerable value, but merely because young men study it. There is no greater respect now than formerly for the ancient languages; in all likelihood there is even less. Doubtless there is good enough ground for this, because the smattering which the ordinary college graduate possesses is not worthy of great appreciation. The main reason for this demand is, after all, a reason of defiance, of insistence upon outward forms, of proving that there is and ought to be no distinction between one person and another, between men and women.

But in spite of disadvantages such as have been alluded to, there has been one step of immense importance, one stride in the right direction. With the competition by women in industrial markets, the necessity of careful and exact preparation for the work in hand has to a certain extent received recognition. The world has always recognized this in regard to men, who unconsciously and as a matter of course follow the idea in their training for active life. From the highest to the lowest, they expect to obtain a logical preparation for a certain work before entering upon its duties; and so radical is this necessity supposed to be that the man who disregards it would in many cases suffer both legal and social penalties. The engineer who tried to run a locomotive without a proper training and knowledge, the physician who undertook the treatment of disease, the dressmaker who risked the value of the customer's materials, the architect who dared to build structures that might endanger other people's lives and money, — these, or any other workers, who assume responsibilities for which they are not fitted, have been and are severely punished for their lack of preparation and the recklessness of their undertakings. Moreover, in proportion to the importance of the interests at stake have the punishments — both legal and social — been set. It accords with conceptions of justice that responsibilities should not be undertaken without good reason for believing that there is a sufficient basis of capability present upon which to base the prospect of approximately fair success.

Here is one of the greatest faults in our methods of preparing women for active life; and in this respect their preparation still differs radically from that of their brothers. A young man's training is a combination of utility and decoration, with the elements of utility in predominance. The sentiment for the greater claims of utility has been so strongly insisted upon that there has been danger of losing sight of the value of the cultural element. In the education of young women the opposite is still held, even where the "higher" education has asserted itself. Here, the principal object seems to be an elaboration of the old-time aim,—an ambition to give the young woman an intellectual experience that is distinctive, unusual, characteristic of luxury rather than utility. A young man's training is designed to further his ability to accomplish definite work in the world; his sister's is still arranged on the plan of making her appear better cared for, more advantageously placed, better apparelled in mental garments than her neighbors. There is little or no view of a finer preparation for a life work, of augmenting her real utility in the world. Therefore, it is quite natural that when, on account of necessity or choice, she attempts to broaden her horizon, the only way that seems open to her is in some industrial pursuit by which she comes into competition with her brother, and divides with him the possible money-rewards of the business world.

In spite of the fact that women have taken upon themselves so many new activities, in spite of the fact that they are often capable of earning a respectable wage, one is met by the strange fact that their efforts have not, on the whole, brought greater ease and physical comfort to the working part of the community. Competition is severer than before, the struggle to exist is fiercer than ever before. Not only is it said that the rich are getting richer and the poor poorer, but also it is claimed that a greater amount of exertion than in former times is necessary to keep up the standard of the great middle class, the real foundation of the social fabric. The question consequently arises, whether the new activities of women pay; whether the world is really the better for their change of condition. Many practically minded people answer this in the negative, claiming that for every woman who obtains a position which a man formerly held, the family that is dependent upon the man's exertions is left, temporarily at least, without the means of livelihood. Moreover, they add, the influx of women into an industry is the signal for decrease in wages. They go on to explain that this fall in wages results from the facts that women have fewer burdens, that they use less judgment in their work than men, and that, since they remain in their positions only until they have a satisfactory opportunity to marry, they are less permanent. While marriage means greater steadiness and reliability in the man, in the woman it means resignation from the position to which she has become trained. For such and other allied reasons, it is held, she is from the beginning less valuable potentially to her employers than the male competitor.

But a further consideration arises which overshadows the action and the fate of the woman who partly or wholly earns her own living. The large majority of women of all sorts marry. They do this because it seems to them and the world their highest place and function, where they will be of most worth to themselves and the community. The mere fact that in this way a woman comes to have a controlling voice in a household, that in her hands lies the making or unmaking of her children's careers, that being the centre of a household she becomes the centre of a widely radiating influence, — all this is a matter of supreme importance. It is unnecessary to demonstrate that her position as wife and mother is the highest which she could possibly attain. Not only has the world done that most thoroughly, but also nature has definitely provided against any refutation of it. Thereupon the question follows, whether the course of modern effort and modern training has raised the general standard of her efficiency as a wife and mother. The whole matter resolves itself into an inquiry concerning the requirements in ability to which a woman who wishes to embody a high type of wife and mother must answer. Even more may the subject be simplified; for, since the maternal duties include and overweigh the uxorial, the natural conclusion must be that the woman who best knows how to rear her children is the one who occupies the highest place in the world; the inquiry may then be confined to the ideas and methods of best attaining this end. One would suppose, in this age of universal improvements, of changing customs, that matters of so much importance would be the first in the mind of every woman, especially every mother. The methods of past times, with their burdensome decorations, are nowadays treated with so little reverence and have been so much developed into the methods of to-day that without thought the conclusion would hold that the children of this time should have a wiser regimen than their ancestors at a like age; and likewise that the women of to-day ought to show a better discipline, a wider scope of view, a wiser application of right principles in the performance of their higher duties than ever before.

Therefore, one is surprised to find that the expected improvement in this most important function does not exist. In other respects women have undoubtedly made progress. They have been energetic enough in assimilating ideas in intellectual and artistic culture, in politics, in the matter of their "rights," in business. But this very energy, instead of inducing a cognate energy in the line of maternal duties, seemingly has turned their attention from them. By a strange lack of logic, they have not applied to this subject their acquired conceptions of the necessity of training and discipline, so that a young woman unhesitatingly assumes the greatest responsibilities with no further preparation than her grandmother possessed. What is even sadder is that there is no perception of the necessity of such preparation. Thus a girl is graduated from school, having a smattering of literature, languages, music, grammar, mathematics, which have not been taught in their physiological order nor in a manner to give the best amount of normal mental exercise, and straightway considers herself competent to have the complete charge, the fullest authority, the main decision in all matters of health and development, physical training and spiritual culture of the children who may in the natural order of things become her offspring. When on account of weakness, indolence, social duties, or what she considers the dignity of her position, she feels that some or all of the care of the child should be taken off her hands, she hires some strange girl or woman, usually of the social and intellectual grade of the peasant, to act as a sort of foster-mother. If this foster-mother, by whatever means she may know, is able to keep the child quiet, if she does not too palpably abuse him, if she tells him any and all sorts of tales,—no matter what her language, her superstitions, or her unformed ideas may be,—she is considered a fit and able nurse, who is doing everything that the parents can reasonably ask of her.

If this seems a harsh characterization, scrutiny will show that it is not overdrawn. Indeed, the mother herself, in many ways, presents no great improvement upon it. Whatever training she may have had has not been of the kind to realize or cope with the problems which are bound to confront her. These problems are matters of physiology, psychology, hygiene, biology. And because they are called by long names does not lessen their importance. And not only is a knowledge of these subjects necessary, but also it is desirable that one should cultivate the state of mind which makes a useful consideration of them easy and natural. The method of thought which one must use in dealing with them requires no unusual power of mind; but it does call for a fair amount of regulated thought, of discipline, of willingness to abide by a definite and logical relation of cause and effect. These are elements which, unfortunately, the ordinary young woman, in attempting to fulfil her maternal duties, is not prepared to use.

In the first place, she should have some idea of the groundwork of biology. She should be acquainted with the natural history of animal forms; she should know something of the wonderful development of cell life; she should be able to understand the rudimentary laws, at least, of the correlation of organic forces. Such things are absolutely essential to a knowledge of the multitudinous influences which go to make up the sum of the child's nutrition, to the building up or the tearing down of the minute cells which in their complexity make up the completed mind and body. Here is a study which is more than interesting — it is even fascinating, which abounds in romantic interest, which carries with it a careful and patient exercise of the reasoning faculty that is of prime importance. There is the same need of this knowledge as there is of the foundations upon which the superstructure of any profession is raised. As well might an architect be ignorant of the minute and gross characteristics of the stone which he uses, or a manufacturer of the raw materials of which his products are made. Not otherwise is one able to know the full meaning of physical life, — how it begins, continues and decays. Surely not otherwise can a mother know how to care for the wonderful development of the infant whose whole life depends upon her knowledge and foresight. If she were able to note the marvellous growth and changes in the tender cotyledons of a plant, the sensitive demeanor of the blood-corpuscles in a frog's circulation, the occurrence of chlorophyl granules and the changes which their presence brings, she certainly would be in a better position to appreciate the workings of her baby's body, more able intelligently to encourage favorable and discourage unfavorable influences. Her sense of the importance, the sacredness of trust which her relationship puts upon her would be vastly increased. And as a result, her duties would be ever so much better performed.

At the same time, a thorough knowledge of physiology is fully as essential. If the same amount of time that is now devoted to the stupefying study of grammar, of the battles of some ancient war-lord whose main claim to distinction was a faculty for oppressing and killing off the peasantry on his lands, of the intricate casuistries of so-called mental and moral philosophy, were given to an understanding of the functions for the human body, its methods of reaction and the phenomena of its metabolism, the benefits of the change would be too great to be easily computed. This change would mean a knowledge of what most, rather than of what least, concerns one. Comparing great things with small, it would be analogous to the relative importance of knowing, on the one hand, all the necessary details of one's household, upon which the comfort, health and happiness of the inmates rest, and, on the other, of being acquainted with the petty political vicissitudes of a remote South American city. In making such a choice there is no doubt on which side any sensible person should stand. And likewise, in an impartially considered scheme of education for a girl, there is as little uncertainty concerning the value of the study of physiology. When the girl becomes a mother, she would not be apt, in the most important matters of life, to depend upon the ignorance of a nurse-maid, the garrulous superstition of uninformed neighbors, or the ofttimes partial and one-sided instruction of her attending physician, who, on account of her very ignorance, is unable to give more than incomplete instruction. With a proper education she would know the meaning of the words *food* and *sleep;* she would know something of their overwhelming importance upon the future being and career of her child, who in his turn is to be one of the world's citizens, with full capacity for good and evil. Knowing what were normal functions, she would be able to recognize and guard against deviations from them. No day would pass in which she would not find opportunity to exercise self-restraint, keen observation and sensible knowledge in furthering the normal and healthful evolution of her child. In proportion to her approximation to a really high standard, this evolution ought to stand for her as the greatest thing in the world.

If the laws governing the body are of so much importance, those controlling the mental action are fully as worthy of consideration. To know how the mind works, the order of its unfolding, the relative importance of the various elements which go to make a nice equilibrium,—these things are of no little value. In the presence of a knowledge of psychology, there would not be so much confusion as to what children should learn, hear and see. The probable effect of the various experiences in life would not be so problematical, and a greater freedom in relation would exist between child and parent. At the same time, an intelligent supervision of the processes of growth, the gradual unfolding of the little one's mind, would be exceedingly stimulating to the mother. It would weightily impress her with the nascent possibilities of her child, with the responsibilities which she has taken upon her, with the solemn import of life. How vastly superior would this be to a frittering away of time in acquiring intellectual decorations and trimmings; in learning valueless pieces of music, especially, as in most cases, when there is no likelihood or possibility of real artistic excellence; of obtaining a cursory and unhomogeneous acquaintance with literature. Such a better knowledge would promote the mother's authority, and strengthen the child's feeling of respect. Not only would she be better able to deal with the varying phases of the budding mind, but also she would be able to foresee what those phases would be apt to be, their rightful interpretation, their relative importance and their imperative needs in treatment. In the face of this information, she would rightly regard herself as having some claim on the respect which ought to be attached to the proud name of mother, on the prerogatives and privileges which belong to the noblest vocation in life.

In addition to this, she must recognize that her duties, while partly philosophical, also have their practical side. The little body that is absolutely in her power and care must be fed and nurtured, must receive the physical materials upon which it works in order to elaborate bone and muscle and nerve tissue. These materials should be so prepared as to give the maximum amount of return in strength for the minimum amount of energy expended in converting them for the uses of the organism. Thus the question of food becomes one of basal importance. The mother should thoroughly know the constitution of the usual articles of diet, their chemical value, what elements of strength each is capable of giving and the differential distinctions between them. She should know not only their ordinary methods of preparation, but also the reasons for these methods, their respective values, and their proper effect upon the general economy. Such a knowledge of applied chemistry is certainly not over-difficult of acquirement, is easily obtained in the time usually devoted to the ordinary school work, especially in the more advanced grades, and at the same time has all the advantages of intellectual exercise which girls now receive. It undoubtedly has as many of these advantages as political economy — as now taught — can give, as proficiency in the Delsartean system, or as practice in sketching and painting can give. It would confer more of intrinsic value instead of extrinsic attraction. A girl thus taught might have less coquetry, less of the art of simpering delicacy, less of the fallacious faculty of casual fascination. But on the other hand, she would be able to order her child's nourishment to the end of conserving all the actual and potential energy of which he is capable, she would be able to provide an intelligent method of restoring wasted tissue, she would know how to supply the easiest means of adding new materials from which new elements may grow. Under such a regime there would be fewer complaints of reflex nervous disorders depending upon an irritated gastro-intestinal system and malassimilation of food. And with these reflex conditions removed, a fertile cause of serious mental and nervous irregularities would simultaneously vanish.

Besides this, the whole growth of the body and the interdependence of its various parts would be more even, more nicely balanced. It is true that the mental maturity might not come so rapidly, but this, instead of being a disadvantage, would act as an advantage; for one should remember that a too rapid maturity is apt to be pathological or, at least, productive of one-sidedness. Parents rarely realize how much the question of diet has to do with the normal, healthy tone of their children's minds, how closely it concerns their peacefulness, their cheerfulness, their temperateness, their susceptibility to legitimate influence. Many a time a close observer will notice an intimate connection between vicious traits and a vicious diet. And a woman who clearly understands the methods and *rationale* of preparing and combining foods is apt to do more real good than any physician by reconstructive measures can hope to accomplish. If to such an understanding she adds an equal acquaintance with the common and known truths of hygiene, her worth to herself, her family and the community will be tremendously increased. By such information she would protect the family health, she would make the general environment more conducive to a clear functional activity. In some schools at the present time a subject called "hygiene" is taught; but its treatment is so slight and unpractical that its value is almost naught. Under a better system the student would really be benefited. She would be able intelligently to discriminate between proper and improper methods of clothing, between proper and improper systems of ventilation, between healthful and harmful physical surroundings. Such a woman could never be guilty of so elementary a matter as allowing a child to run about in cold weather wearing short socks, leaving a portion of the leg exposed to the risk of congestive influences; she would know what were the demands of sufficient drainage and plumbing; she would have some idea of the value of a scientific cleanliness. By her knowledge of such matters as the conduction of heat, of the requirements of a healthful and sufficient water supply, she would promote the comfort and well-being of those who were dependent upon her guarding care.

Such studies might advantageously form part of a training which would infinitely promote the health, prosperity and right development of the community. They would convert a great body of more or less useless women into most valuable workers. That some change in occupation and training is necessary there can be no doubt. And the well-known restlessness, dissatisfaction and discontent of modern women is one proof of it. An increasing number of them complain continually of seeing no object in life, of having nothing to work for, of having no goal by which to guide their ways. Unquestionably a reason for this is the fact that the old ideas are passing away. There is a common consciousness that old-time methods may be made better, that women are as susceptible of improvement in their ways as men are. They have felt and are feeling more acutely than ever the controlling spirit of the time which is revolutionary, iconoclastic, sceptical of rule-of-thumb methods by which our ancestors were guided. One can easily imagine why it is that the large body of women are striving for normal activity, are trying to secure by any manner of means a release from an environment which makes them inferiors of their fathers, husbands and brothers. The reason is in large part based on the feeling that their sphere of work is somewhat trivial, that their range of influence is not important enough for their dignity. Under a better custom things would change. Rather would they then look upon themselves as different, not inferior. They would recognize that the difference between men and women is a matter of mental and physical constitution. And a difference in constitution means a difference in function. When this becomes clearly known, when women feel within themselves the responsibilities of definite and useful activity and with this recognize the normal and right field for their abilities, there will be less of an outcry against the "unnatural competition" between brother and sister, husband and wife. The more clearly each one recognizes his limitations and proper field of endeavor, the sooner will a more tolerable condition of affairs come about. And as soon as their recognition is definite and clear cut, there will grow up in women as in men, a triumphant demand for the best preparation that will fit them for their proper activity.

The world has always recognized that a woman's natural and highest sphere is that of mother, and the woman who best embodied the mother-ideal has always been the subject of the sincerest worship. In the changes incident to modern life the fact that the means for attaining this ideal may be altered has been lost sight of. As a result of historical experience, women have been in the habit of looking upon maternity too much in the light of an incident, as an accident of life which may come as sickness or revolution in affairs may come, and for which no adequate preparation (outside of a financial preparation) can or need be made. But nowadays we know better than that; we know that when a woman has the opportunity of putting herself in an environment which has always and must always represent the highest point in her ambitions, when as a result of this she assumes responsibilities which transcend in importance those of almost any profession or calling, when we know that these responsibilities may be wisely or unwisely administered, and that there is a large range of subjects which can rightly form the basis of preparation for administering them, then one may say that in such work lies the finest vocation that a mounting ambition could desire. One must say that in the profession of maternity lies the hope of the time, the cure for the restlessness, the discontent and the chagrin that torment the feminine world. One may rightly call it a cure, because it not only provides a method of absorption of restless energy, giving an outlet for the exercise of every faculty of which a woman is capable, but also because it has for its object the highest aim toward which men have ever cast their eyes: the betterment of the individual and the race.

However, the absorption of restlessness is really a secondary matter. The main consideration is, that any woman has a right to look forward to making a career in the world for herself, and that this right is founded upon much the same grounds which support the anticipations for a life work of her brother. So long as one recognizes this, one must likewise recognize the necessity of ascertaining in what directions the girl's possibilities tend, what her sphere of greatest usefulness really is, and what the best means of culture therein are. So long as she is considered capable of filling the noble position of a mother, so long as there is a hope of her assuming its duties and obligations, the question about the choice of a vocation for her has simultaneously been answered. Lamentations concerning the "unsexing of women by stress of industrial life," concerning the ruinous competition between men and women, would have no reason for existence. It must be evident that the ideal industrial condition is obtained, not so much by putting each person in a cutting competition with his neighbor, but by so regulating opportunities that every one has the work for which he is best designed. So far as women are concerned, there is little or no attempt at the present to do this. Whatever training they obtain is usually of the most general kind. This in itself is sad enough; but what is still worse is that no idea of the seriousness of the deficiency is generally appreciated. If a similar conception in regard to any one of the recognized trades or professions were held, one would be justified in believing that the occupation could not possibly be of much importance. Therefore, it is quite remarkable that, in the matter of the most vital trust which can be reposed upon a human being, thoughtful and conscientious persons should not long ago have recognized the necessities of the case, and after recognizing them insisted upon a proper provision for answering them. The facts that women are from the beginning designed especially for the profession of maternity, that by following it they best fulfil all their physical and mental functions, and that the paramount value of this work is plain and clear, make the claims of this vocation upon our respectful consideration exceedingly strong. So long as this is true, the conclusion must follow that the main part of the preparatory training of girls, even though the present customs and ideals be thereby wholly altered, should be formed upon what the requirements of the main work in her life dictate. When the premises are once admitted, it is nothing less than wanton neglect and stultification to deny in any part the inevitable conclusion.

The change in the educational life of woman here indicated is so radical from what is now in vogue, that one may be apt to think it chimerical, that women will always insist on having a large decorative element in their training. To set the doubt at rest one need merely call to mind the changed standards of customs and living which have occurred in the last few years.

The very life of women in numberless details has changed so much that our grandmothers would never have been able to imagine the conditions of their descendants. Even in far other matters, even where the controlling force is as rigorous and inevitable as commercial demands, the spirit of the time insists so strikingly on progress and so sharply stimulates endeavor, that what was impossible yesterday becomes to-day not only possible, but commonplace. Not so many years ago Herbert Spencer, in writing about the limitations of human work and knowledge, said: "Numerous attempts have been made to construct electro-magnetic engines, in the hope of superseding steam; but had those who supplied the money understood the general law of the correlation and equivalence of forces, they might have had better balances at their bankers." When this sentence was written the futility of the scheme in question seemed so apparent that even a man like Spencer, a man of great knowledge, wisdom and scientific imagination, could see nothing more in the idea of superseding steam by electricity than a wild project that sober minds could never entertain. Nevertheless, such motors are in use to-day, are successfully run, and bid fair in time to abolish the use of steam.

Ever so much more easily could the view-points in the education of women be altered. Not only are women amenable to the change, but also they would welcome it as deliverance from the reputed intellectual bondage in which so many of them believe that they are held. In addition, the quality of the time demands the change. What women are asking for is not so much an increase in ease and luxury, an increase in the decorative and fantastic elements in life; on the contrary, more than ever before, I believe, do they long for a high grade of usefulness, for the possibility of making a career for themselves. Such an ambition, capable of all nobility, striving and self-sacrifice, can never be gratified under the conditions of our present education. The elements of satisfying such emotions do not in large enough degree exist. But under conditions which would bring about an immeasurable uplifting in the standards of physical, mental and spiritual existence, there could be no limit to the useful work which would lie at their hands. Under such auspices, marriage would become easier, its disabilities lighter, its reasons stronger than ever. Much of the present "unnatural competition" would have no reason for existence and so would cease to exist. The community would have more time in which to live, for the time, effort and value that are consumed by faulty methods of management would act as clear gain. Not the least among the advancing steps of the age will be the recognition of the duties, the emoluments and the comparative value of maternity, and when the preparation for it assumes the dignity of a professional training and the fulfilment of its obligations and possibilities, the best ideal of a fine career, the world must see that it has taken a great stride along the path of its natural evolution.

INDEX

Abdominal aorta, relation in size to common iliac arteries, 42.
Alberson, 149.
Alveoli of lungs, 42, 43.
Amœba, 207.
Amylopsin, 47.
Annulus tympanicus, 26.
Aorta, relation in size to pulmonary artery, 41.
Apes, platyrhine, 30.
Aristotle, 93.
Aryans, 124.
Atlas, 32.

Bacchic orgies, 129.
Bacon, 93.
Baer, 177.
Basi-occipital bone, 22.
Basi-sphenoidal bone, 22.
Beranger, 177.
Best on Evidence, 149.
Bile, 39.
Binswanger, 54.
Bishop, W., 230.
Bladder, 49.
Blind Tom, 217, 230.
Blood, in infants, 17, 18.
  specific gravity of, 17.
Body-plasm, 80.
Bone elements, comparative table of, 16.
Bones, 16.
  development of long, 19.
  Wormian, 177.
Brain, 52, 53.
  cells of, 55.
  convolutions of, 53.

Bramans, origin of, 124.
Bronchi, 42, 43.
Bushmen, African, 217.
  Australian, 132.

Cæcum, 47, 48.
Cæsar, 232.
Cajal, 59.
California system of child-caring, 259.
Camp-meetings, excitement of, 129.
Cartilage, 17.
Cartilages, costal, 33.
Caterpillar, 11, 12.
Celts, origin of, 124.
Cerebellum, 53, 61.
  vermis of, 61.
Chest, proportions of, 34.
Chromatin, 59.
Chronic constipation, 49.
Clavicle, right, 35.
Clavicles, 33.
Clouston, 207.
Coccyx, 51.
Code of criminal procedure, New York state, 150.
Colon, ascending, 47.
  ascending, mesentery of, 48.
  ascending, peritonæum of, 48.
  transverse, 47.
Comenius, 93.
Conus arteriosus, 35.
Corpora quadrigemina, 56.
Corre, 177.
Cranium, comparative dimensions of, 23.
Credulity, natural, 127.
Crime, climate as cause of, 191.

294   INDEX

Crime, destitution as cause of, 180.
    diet as cause of, 192.
    drunkenness as cause of, 181.
    environment as cause of, 193.
    heredity as cause of, 183.
    ignorance as cause of, 178.
    weather as cause of, 192.
Crishna, 125.
Cro-Magnon race, 71.
Cyril, 127.

Darwin, 73.
Dase, 218.
Degeneracy, 238.
Dendron, 58.
Despine, Prosper, 177.
Devaki, 126.
Diana, 127.
Diaphragm, 42.
Diehl, Conrad, 116, 117.
Dionysius, 125.
Dordogne, 71.
Dugdale, 188, 189, 201.
Duodenum, 48.
Dura Mater, 21.

Ear, 25.
Ear drum, 26.
Epiglottis, 32.
Epilepsy, 77.
Erasmus, 93.
Eustachian tube, 26, 27.
    relation to hard palate, 26.

Face, comparative dimensions of, 21, 22.
    growth of, 23.
Fatigue, effects of, in the young, 89.
Fehling, 13.
Femoral artery, 45.
Fermentation, intestinal, 168.
Fetteroff, 264.
Fibrinogen, 18.
Firnald, 221.
Fissure of Rolando, 54.

Fissure of Sylvius, 54.
Flechsig, 56.
Fontanelles, 20.
Foramen cæcum, 21.
Foramen magnum, 23.
Foramen ovale, 36.
Frederick William I., 93.
Frigga, 26.
Froebel, 93, 96, 97, 98, 115, 256.
Frontal bone, orbital plate of, 21.
Frontal sinus, 21.

Gall bladder, 38.
Galton, 67, 146.
Gambara, 177.
Garofalo, 176.
Geggenbühl, 218.
Genius, the, 230, 231.
Germ-plasm, 79.
Girard College, 263.
Glands, Brunner's, 48.
    lachrymal, 25.
    Lieberkühn's, 48.
    prostate, 49.
    ptyalin-forming, 31.
    solitary and agminated, 48.
God, child's conception of, 133, 165.
Goethe, 235.
Goltz, experiments of, 52.
Greeks, origin of, 124.
Greenleaf, on Evidence, 150.
Gundobin, 18.

Hailman, W. N., 99.
Hare-lip, 28.
Heart, "milk spot" of, 36.
    proportions of, 35.
    relation in size to arterial system, 41.
    relation in size to liver, 40.
Hercules, 125.
Herodotus, 126.
Hodge, 53.
Holder, von, 176.
Horus, 127.
Howard, 220.

Infarctions, uric acid, 44.
Inferior turbinated bone, 27.
Ireland, Dr., 214.
Isis, 126.
Italians, origin of, 124.

Jaw, upper, 22.
    upper, ramus of, 24.
Jews, ancient, 123.
    descent of, 71, 72.
Joyce, Dr., 108.
Jukes, 188.

Keilbau, 97.
Kidneys, development of, 44.
Knee joint, development of, 19.

Larynx, 32.
Laurent, 152, 177.
Lavelaye, de, 64.
Liver, development of, 37.
Lombroso, 61.
Longet, experiments of, 52.
Lourdes, 139.
Lowell, Mrs. J. S., 252.
Lymphatic system, 48.

Macula lutea, 25.
Malpighi, pyramids of, 44.
Marimo, 177.
Marrow, 17.
Massachusetts system of child-caring, 258.
Mastoid bone, 19, 20.
Mastoid process, 20.
Maudesley, 122.
Maya-Maya, 126.
Meatus of ear, 26.
Medes and Persians, origin of, 124.
Mediastinum, 32.
Medulla oblongata, 56.
Membrana tympani, 26.
Metteay, 255.
Michigan system of child-caring, 259.
Mithras, 125.

Moral Revival, 1.
Morals, training in, 142.
Morrison, 180, 181, 187.
Mouth, cavity of, 24.
Muscles, 17.

Napoleon, 233.
Nasal cavity, 24.
Naso-pharynx, 24.
Nerve branches, development of, 57.
Nerve cells, functions of, 208, 210, 211.
Neuron, 58.
New Hampshire system of child-caring, 259.
New South Wales, 257.
New York system of child-caring, 258.
Nose, growth of, 27, 28.

Obersteiner, 77.
Occipital bone, union with spheroid bone, 20.
Ogle, 179.
Orbit, 21.
Orbit, relation to nose, 24.
Osiris, 125.
Ossicles, auditory, 25.

Palate, hard, 24.
Palate, soft, 30.
Parker, 128.
Patterson, 150.
Payaguas, 132.
Perinæum, 50.
    fasciæ of, 50.
Pestalozzi, 93, 96, 97, 256.
Petro-squamous suture, 20.
Pons varolii, 56.
Predisposition, 75, 76.
Prenated diseases, 76.
Prenatal impressions, 78.
Preyer, 61.
Protozoa, 68.
Psychical trauma, 170.
Ptyalin, 31.
Purkinje, cells of, 53.

INDEX

Ranke, 226.
Recessus opticus, 25.
Rectum, 48, 49.
    peritonæum, 49.
    prolapse of, 49.
Renin, 47.
Ribs, 33, 34.
Richardson, Mrs., 260.
Richter, 177.
Robinson, L., 60.
Russell, 135, 156.

Sachs, 209.
Secrétan, M. Charles, 2.
Seguin, 213, 217, 219.
Semele, 126.
Sernoff, 54.
Serum, specific gravity of, 17.
Shamanism, 129.
Shuttleworth, 213.
Sigmoid flexure, 47, 48.
Siva worship, 129.
Skull, comparative dimensions of, 23.
Slavonic nations, origin of, 124.
Socrates, 93.
Soubirous, Bernadette, 139.
Spencer, Herbert, 100, 290.
Sphenoidal sinus, 21.
Sphenoid bone, union with occipital bone, 20.
Sphincter, œsophageal, 46.
Spine, 50, 51.
Spleen, 39.
Steapsin, 47.
Sternum, 32, 33.
Stomach, development of, 46.

Taylor, on Evidence, 151.
Teeth —
    bicuspids, 29.
    canines, 29.
    incisors, 29.
    molars, 29.
    molar, fourth, 30.

Teeth —
    alveolar processes of, 28.
    coronoid processes of, 29.
    development of, 28, 29.
    milk, 29.
Temporal bone, parietal portion of, 24; squamous portion of, 23.
Terra del Fuegians, 132.
Tertullian, 126.
Teutons, 70.
Thymus gland, 31.
Thyroid gland, 32.
Tongue, development of, 30; follicles of, 31.
Tonsil, pharyngeal, 31.
Trachea, 33.
Tragus of ear, 26.
Trypsin, 47.
Tuberculosis, debilitating effects of, 213, 214; transmission of, 76.
Tympanum (middle ear), 21.

Urethra, 49.
Uterus, 49.
Uvula, 31.

Victoria, 257.
Vierordt's table of comparative percentages, 15.
Vision in new-born child, 25.
Vomer, 23.

Wagner, 234.
Warner, 198.
Washington, 233.
Water, proportion of, in fœtus, 13.
Wharton, 151.
Whitwell, 226.
Whirling dervishes, 129.
Wichern, 255.

Yverdun, 96, 97.

Zygomata (cheek bones), 23.

THE STUDY OF CHILDREN AND THEIR SCHOOL TRAINING.

By FRANCIS WARNER, M.D.

12mo. Cloth. Price $1.00, net.

A practical book. The conclusions are based on FACTS, not theories, gained by Dr. Warner from the examinations of 100,000 school children. Parents and teachers are shown *what* observations to make and *how* to make them. Suggestions for overcoming many puzzling difficulties are given. No more valuable book for those interested in the study of children has been published.

"This is a volume singularly clear and exact in its expression and definite in its generalization, the first really scientific monograph on child study that we have in any language. We believe that the publication of this volume will exert a profound and far-reaching influence for good in aiding teachers and parents in doing the best that can be done with children in various phases in life." — *Journal of Pedagogy.*

"I am greatly pleased with the book, and I believe it will be of marked benefit to teachers in all grades of educational work. I trust it may find its way into the hands of a great many teachers and parents, for I feel it is of genuine merit, combining scientific and practical qualities in a happy manner." — Prof. M. B. O'SHEA, *University of Wisconsin.*

"I regard this volume as one of the very best contributions yet made on the subject of Child Study." — J. M. GREENWOOD, *Supt. of City Schools, Kansas City, Mo.*

"This book seems to us an extremely suggestive and important one for teachers and parents; and being simply written, and free from technicalities, it may be understood and applied with ease by any reader." — *The Dial.*

"The physical side of child development which has been frequently ignored is here presented in a very forcible and practical manner. The book will be most valuable to Kindergartners, and to all, mothers and teachers and students, who are interested in Child Study." — Miss HILDA JOHNSON, *President of Kindergarten Union, N. Y. City.*

"The Study of Children is a most valuable book that should have a very large circulation. Parents will find it most helpful, for it contains a mass of the most valuable material dealing with the health and training of children. It is an original, strong, and thoroughly satisfactory work." — *Boston Saturday Evening Gazette.*

"There is no better statement than is here given of the way to study a child. Dr. Warner tells what to look for and what to look at." — *Journal of Education.*

"The book is indispensable to the teacher's library, and is full of information for those who are engaged in directing education, philanthropy, social settlement work, as well as any student of mental development." — *Child Study Monthly.*

"The Study of Children and their School Training is one of the most valuable contributions yet made to the literature of scientific education. It contains information of interest to all who are intelligently awake to the progress of educational movement and other forms of social work connected with mental science." — *Philadelphia Evening Telegraph.*

THE MACMILLAN COMPANY,
66 FIFTH AVENUE, NEW YORK.

MENTAL DEVELOPMENT

IN

THE CHILD AND THE RACE.

BY

JAMES MARK BALDWIN, M.A., Ph.D.,

With Seventeen Figures and Ten Tables. 8vo. pp. xvi, 496. Cloth.
Price, $2.60.

FROM THE PRESS.

"It is of the greatest value and importance." — *The Outlook.*

"A most valuable contribution to biological psychology." — *The Critic.*

"Thorough, candid, and suggestive : in thorough touch with the researches of the day." — *The Week* (Toronto, Canada).

"Professor Baldwin has treated in this book a subject that is new and full of absorbing interest. . . . Many will find Professor Baldwin's book stimulating." — *The American Journal of Psychology.*

"An exceedingly valuable book, and will be read with great interest by teachers, cultured parents, and psychologists." — *Popular Science News.*

"This summary sketch can give no idea of the variety of topics which Professor Baldwin handles, or of the originality with which his central thesis is worked out. No psychologist can afford to neglect the book." — *The Dial.*

"The first real successful effort at a presentation of the psychological process from the genetic point of view — the central idea of the growing, developing being." — *The Child-Study Monthly.*

"A book . . . treating of a subject fraught with significant revelations for every branch of educational science is Professor J. Mark Baldwin's treatise on Mental Development in 'The Child and the Race.' Professor Baldwin's work is comparatively untechnical in character and written in a terse and vigorous style, so that it will commend itself to unprofessional readers. The educational, social, and ethical implications, in which the subject abounds, the author has reserved for a second volume, which is well under way ; the present treats of methods and processes. Having been led by his studies and experiments with his two little daughters to a profound appreciation of the genetic function of imitation, he has sought to work out a theory of mental development in the child incorporating this new insight. A clear understanding of the mental development of the individual child necessitates a doctrine of the race development of consciousness — the great problem of the evolution of mind. Accordingly Professor Baldwin has endeavored to link together the current biological theory of organic adaptation with the doctrine of the infant's development as that has been fashioned by his own wide, special researches. Readers familiar with the articles of Professor Haeckel now running in *The Open Court* will understand the import of a theory which seeks to unite and explain one by the other the psychological aspects of ontogenesis and phylogenesis. As Professor Baldwin says, it is the problem of Spencer and Romanes attacked from a new and fruitful point of view. There is no one but can be interested in the numerous and valuable results which Professor Baldwin has recorded; teachers, parents, and psychologists alike will find in his work a wealth of suggestive matter." — *The Open Court.*

THE MACMILLAN COMPANY,

66 FIFTH AVENUE, NEW YORK.

A COURSE OF LECTURES
ON THE
GROWTH AND MEANS OF TRAINING
THE
MENTAL FACULTY.

DELIVERED IN THE UNIVERSITY OF CAMBRIDGE.

BY

FRANCIS WARNER, M.D. (Lond.),
F.R.C.P., F.R.C.S. (Eng.),

Physician to the London Hospital; Lecturer on Therapeutics and on Botany at the London Hospital College; Formerly Hunterian Professor of Anatomy and Physiology in the Royal College of Surgeons of England.

12mo. Cloth. Price, 90 cents, net.

NOTICES.

"It is original, thorough, systematic, and wonderfully suggestive. Every superintendent should study this book. Few works have appeared lately which treat the subject under consideration with such originality, vigor, or good sense." — *Education.*

"A valuable little treatise on the physiological signs of mental life in children, and on the right way to observe these signs and classify pupils accordingly. . . . The book has great originality, and though somewhat clumsily put together, it should be very helpful to the teacher on a side of his work much neglected by the ordinary treatises on pedagogy." — *Literary World.*

"The eminence and experience of the author, and the years of careful study he has devoted to this and kindred subjects, are a sufficient guarantee for the value of the book; but those who are fortunate enough to examine it will find their expectations more than fulfilled. . . . A great deal may be learned from these lectures, and we strongly commend them to our readers." — *Canada Educational Journal.*

THE MACMILLAN COMPANY,
66 FIFTH AVENUE, NEW YORK.

AN OUTLINE OF PSYCHOLOGY.

BY

EDWARD BRADFORD TITCHENER, A.M., Ph.D.,
Sage Professor of Psychology at the Cornell University.

Second Edition with Corrections.

8vo. Cloth. $1.50, net.

"As a contribution both able and useful, Professor Titchener's volume will unquestionably find, as it deserves, a most cordial welcome. In many ways it is the most serviceable text-book of psychology from a modern scientific point of view that has been written. The author is an experimentalist, but clings to the special interpretation of certain fundamental principles which is characteristic of Wundt and his disciples. The result of this definite position is to make the work clear, exact in expression, systematic, methodical. The work is thoroughly good and useful."—JOSEPH JASTROW, *University of Wisconsin*, in the *Dial*.

A PRIMER OF PSYCHOLOGY.

BY

EDWARD BRADFORD TITCHENER,
M.A. (Oxon.), Ph.D. (Leipzig),
Sage Professor of Psychology in the Cornell University.

12mo. Cloth.

This volume is intended as a first book in psychology. It will therefore seek to accomplish the two main ends of a scientific primer of the subject; to outline, with as little of technical detail as is compatible with accuracy of statement, the methods and most important results of modern psychology, and to furnish the reader with references for further study. It will be written with direct regard to the courses of psychological instruction offered in Normal Schools and High Schools, but will at the same time be made sufficiently comprehensive to give the general student a fair idea of the present status of psychology in its various branches.

A novel feature of the work will be the emphasis laid on the experimental method. A short list of simple and inexpensive apparatus will be given, with directions for their use in the class-room, and the experiments described will be such as can be performed by their aid or by help of others that can readily be constructed by the teacher himself. Diagrams, psychological not physiological in character, will be freely used in illustration of the text.

THE MACMILLAN COMPANY,
66 FIFTH AVENUE, NEW YORK.

THE CHILD AND CHILDHOOD
IN FOLK-THOUGHT.

(The Child in Primitive Culture.)

Studies of the Activities and Influences of the Child among Primitive Peoples, their Analogues and Survivals in the Civilization of To-day.

BY

ALEXANDER FRANCIS CHAMBERLAIN, M.A., Ph.D.,

Lecturer on Anthropology in Clark University, Worcester, Mass.; etc., etc

8vo. Cloth. $3.00, net.

"It is an exhaustive study of "child thought" in all ages, and will fully interest every class of students in child study. . . . The teacher of kindergarten will find texts of value upon every page of the book." — *Chicago Inter-Ocean.*

"It is, of course, keenly interesting. One can turn to the copious index and select a topic here, topic there, turn to pages indicated, and find a wonderful amount of information drawn from authentic sources by patient scientific investigation. This investigation covers the entire range of childhood, child life, child care, and child development." — *Buffalo Commercial.*

"The author is an anthropologist, whose dominant interest and training are the philology, rites, customs, and beliefs of primitive people. The book is the first and only one of the kind in English, and is sure to fascinate parents of young children as well as to instruct all teachers and psychologists. It marks a distinct advance in child study." — *American Journal of Psychology.*

"Not the least valuable thing about the book is its suggestiveness. There is hardly a section that does not furnish a subject for detailed investigation to the anthropological psychologist." — *Mind.*

THE MACMILLAN COMPANY,
66 FIFTH AVENUE, NEW YORK.

www.ingramcontent.com/pod-product-compliance
Lightning Source LLC
Chambersburg PA
CBHW031903220426
43663CB00006B/742